Philip A. Verhalen

Religion is a Personal Matter

PETER LANG

New York • Bern • Frankfurt am Main • Paris

Library of Congress Cataloging-in-Publication Data

Verhalen, Philip A.
   Religion is a personal matter : by Philip A.
Verhalen.
   p. cm. – (American university studies. Series
XIV, Education ; vol. 29)
   Includes bibliographical references.
   1. Religion. I. Title. II. Series.
BL48.V45   1990   200–dc20   89-28144
ISBN 0-8204-1195-7   CIP
ISSN 0740-4565

CIP-Titelaufnahme der Deutschen Bibliothek

Verhalen, Philip A.:
Religion is a personal matter / Philip A. Verha-
len. – New York; Bern; Frankfurt am Main;
Paris: Lang, 1990.
  (American University Studies: Ser. 14,
Education; Vol. 29)
  ISBN 0-8204-1195-7

NE: American University Studies / 14

© Peter Lang Publishing, Inc., New York 1990

Printed by Weihert-Druck GmbH, Darmstadt, West Germany

Religion is a Personal Matter

American University Studies

Series XIV
Education
Vol. 29

PETER LANG
New York • Bern • Frankfurt am Main • Paris

To Kathy

Mulier fortis uxorque amabilis

Acknowledgements

My academic indebtedness is documented in many parts of the text and notes. Yet much of my profound personal debt is to friends, relatives and colleagues who have been close to me during the times of pressure and puzzlement, sifting and sorting, shaping and reworking.

My special appreciation endures for the advice of Darrell Reeck of The University of Puget Sound, Bernard Prusak of Villanova University and Mike Barre of St. Patrick's Seminary, Menlo Park. For practical and academic support I wish to thank John Cobb Jr. of The Claremont Graduate School of Theology, Dale Turner of "The Seattle Times" and Dave McCloskey and John Bean, both of Seattle University. Finally I note the person central to this review of support and encouragement, my dear wife and closest friend, Kathy. ·

Contents

Preface

In love, in art, in avarice, in politics, in labor, in games
we study to utter our painful secret.

The man is only half himself,
the other half is his expression.

(from "The Poet" by Ralph Waldo Emerson)

Since I was a small boy I wondered why some people seemed to be more religious than others, and why certain acts appeared to be more religious than others. As I grew older I felt myself yearning to intensify my individuality and I further wondered: Does this endanger my relationship with God? Finally upon completion of my book *Faith in a Secularized World*, the questions of students and forces within the institutional church nudged me to inquire more resolutely into the basic questions that any alert person would ask in his or her quest for growth in personal belief systems and value systems. What followed was a delightful journey beginning with a year at Claremont's Graduate School of Theology (1975-76). At the direction of John Cobb Jr., I related basic questions about religion to contemporary discussions about God in Process Theology. Then intermittently, between 1977 and the present, I returned to this effort with the special assistance of students and friends as I taught this material at Pacific Lutheran University, the University of Puget Sound and Seattle University.

If half of me is expression I sense an experience of personal discovery in all I write. Emerson prompted me to look once again at each chapter. To my surprise I found myself, my experience, my questions in each chapter; nevertheless, I persisted in demanding that there be objective content of value and interest for any person who lives in our times and culture.

Throughout the discussion of human values and the power and destiny of human life it seems hardly insignificant that we distinguish the life of the individual person from that of the community. In 1948 Albert Camus addressed the Dominicans at the Monastery of Latour-Maubourg. Central to his speech about optimism and pessimism for the future of the world was his statement:

> Christians and communists will tell me that their optimism is based on a longer range, that it is superior to all the rest, and that God or history according to the individual is the satisfying end product of their dialectic. I can indulge in the same reasoning. If Christianity is pessimistic as to man, it is optimistic as to human destiny. Well, I can say that, pessimistic as to human destiny, I am optimistic as to man.[1]

Camus, although faintly, distinguished man as an individual person, and a numerical entity that stood in temporal contrast with human destiny. Once we multiply individual persons we have a community - for good or ill - and we have a representation on a more clearly defined historical grid of mankind. If religion is related to persons and religious values are investigated on a personal basis, we rise to ask how religious values affect the individual in contrast with the community at large. In brief, how am I a religious person if my individuality and my bonds with society at large are distinguished in my personhood?

Federal Way, Washington
1984.

Notes

1 Albert Camus, *Resistance, Rebellion and Death*, (New York: The Modern
Library 1960), pp. 54, 55.

Introduction

The study of religion is fascinating! Yet, this study runs the risk of being less than a scientific study. Before we ask precisely how we define religion we ask: "What is it?" at least in general. If we choose to study all the experiences of religion by all peoples for all times we have so enormous a task that we are shocked into immobility. How do we start? Do we begin with a given religion, or a given age of religion, or a given expression of religion such as rituals, sacrifices, symbols etc.? If we look at one expression of religion or religious activity should we not compare it with other religions or religious activities, and then how do we come to the knowledge of all this material?

Mirecea Eliade faces the problem of the study of religion by focusing first on what people agree is sacred. That which is sacred, and religious in this world is viewed as opposite of the profane and secular life. Yet, as we begin to study what is sacred and what is profane we discover distinct difficulties. Almost all religious phenomena suggest a long historical condition. A thing, place or person becomes sacred only gradually with differing levels of profane qualities remaining.

Once we become immersed in the study of religion we are looking at history, the evolution of cultures and peoples. We compare religious expressions as more or less complex, with changing morphologies and varying expressions. To limit or to define the sacred we must begin with a manageable number of expressions of religion. Practically speaking, we must choose a section of a study from the rites, myths, sacred objects and places, animals, plants, persons, and symbols set in time and space under the initial idea of sacred expression or hierophany.

From the idea of hierophany we begin to see some of the basic characteristics of the study of religion. The hierophany occurs in history and culture and is reflected upon and acted upon by human persons. The study is at once history, cultural anthropology, and sociology, but as we begin to look at the sacred elements of religion as events and facts we enter the arena of phenomenology.

Phenomena of Religion

The religious historian must face not only the history of a given hierophany, but must first of all understand and explain the modality of the sacred that the hierophany discloses. The capacity of religious people to know the different modalities of their sacred expressions is basic to the problem of recording religious history. To interpret the meaning calls for a scholar in a particular religion who sees the phenomena, and unlike some members of a given religion, shows a clear understanding of its chief religious expressions.

The fact that a hierophany is always an historic event does not lessen its universal sense. For instance, some Indians venerate a certain tree called asvattha[1] as the manifestation of the sacred in a particular place and species of plant. But this veneration draws only a limited group of people. Indians also hold the symbol of a cosmic tree (axis mundi) identified with cosmic trees of many ancient cultures. While this asvattha shares in the same symbolism of the cosmic tree, it holds its own meaning as a hierophany for only a given Indian society.

The variety of forms of religion does not pose an obstacle to the understanding of a hierophany. The variety gives us the opportunity to discover all the different modalities of the sacred. A hierophany present in one agricultural rite presupposes the entire system portraying the sacredness of vegetation. The variety gives examples that create patterns which eventually open up meanings of whole sections of religious phenomena.

As the human mind developed it sought to confer meaning on human experiences. Carl Sandburg in "The People will Live On" said:

> Once having marched
> Over the margins of animal necessity,
> Over the grim line of sheer subsistence

Then man came
To the deeper rituals of his bones,
To the lights lighter than any bones,
To the time for thinking things over,
To the dance, the song, the story,
Or the hours given over to dreaming,
Once having so marched.

When this awareness of a real and meaningful world grew, the sacred was discovered. Through the experience of the sacred the human mind distinguished between that which shows itself as real, powerful, rich and meaningful, and that which does not. For Eliade the sacred is a part of the structure of consciousness, not a stage in the history of consciousness. Human life becomes meaningful by searching out the sacred and by imitating the models revealed by supernatural beings. From the most ancient times, the imitation of the gods served as a guideline of human existence. From earliest history we discovered that living as a human being is in itself a religious act. To live, and to grow, and to become means to be a religious person.

All human activity becomes a questing for the sacred. Even in our secularized society considered as a process of demythologizing, we look at a number of apparently non-religious phenomena in which we can decipher new and original recoveries of the sacred (e.g. a housewarming party). Basically, the total person is never completely desacralized, but tends to identify the sacred often hidden in the new and ever changing structures of our society.

Several Approaches

To treat adequately the topic of religion we must be open to several approaches. Chief among these are: the historical approach, the anthropological approach, the sociological approach, the philosophical and theological approach, the psychological approach, and the phenomenological approach. Looking at each category briefly we begin with the historical approach.

The historical approach involves the detailed investigation of source material and the checking of their validity and reliability. Within this historical method the personal bias of the investigative historians must receive special consideration. Depending on the subject area and period of history, the task is more or less difficult to perform. For example, it is quite difficult to investigate all of the source material related to the actual events of the Crusades, but when we go back to the synoptic problem in our investigation of the gospels, the source material and the actual events become more difficult to find and weigh. The historian must estimate the reliability of original writers, eye witnesses and recorders of events. Linguistics as well as psychological considerations enter the picture. For this reason history gradually becomes more closely linked with the behavioral or social sciences.

The anthropological approach, true to the Greek roots of the term, engages itself in the study of man. This study includes human biology, biochemistry, physiology, sociology, psychology and most of the social sciences. In practice however, anthropology limits itself. Traditionally it concentrates on the investigation of primitive tribes - existing and extinct. This study flourishes under two allied categories: ethnography and ethnology. While the study of technologically primitive societies is called ethnography, the anthropological study of socio-economic systems and cultural heritage, especially the factors involving growth and change in technologically primitive societies, is called ethnology.

Ethnography is an empirical science analogous to physics and chemistry for all intents and purposes. Within this discipline is physical anthropology: concerned with biological and genetic development of the human species and culture, social anthropology: concerned with the social structure of primitive societies, and cultural anthropology: often linked to social anthropology as a study of primitive cultures.

A wealth of information about religious customs and beliefs flows from the anthropological studies of primitive cultures. Our understanding of animism, pantheism, totemism and many other primitive religious beliefs finds its source in the scholarship of this discipline.[2] Frazer's *The Golden Bough* (1929) provides us with a classical summary of the work of anthropology in primitive religion. The sociological approach is closely allied to anthropology. Sociology studies the structure and function of modern society. Employing the observation technique of anthropology, sociology also collects information by means of surveys and later subjects this information to statistical analysis. With advanced world communications most existing primitive cultures are no longer isolated and able to provide an uncontaminated source for cultural studies. Consequently, anthropologists use the techniques of sociology to investigate and observe isolated cultures and societies. The mixing of the anthropologist's ethnological system with the sociological system effectively blurs the two disciplines in modern scientific investigations into one image.

The philosophical approach is wisdom-centered. This "love" of wisdom pursues such topics as metaphysics, epistemology, ethics, aesthetics, and logic. Metaphysics is the basis of all philosophy for it strives to unlock the mysteries of existence and pure being, (essence). Philosophy moves back beyond science and its quest for immediate causes, to the first cause of the universe or any element in the universe. Armed with the various philosophical tools for clear reasoning, the philosopher usually brings his interest and expertise into the study of religion. The philosophy of religion treats the origin, nature and value of religion and religious experiences.

By contrast, the theological approach treats of the same subject, but brings to the investigation the content of revelation. Theology as a study of God looks to the revealed material or scriptures of each major religion as proceeding from the "God" of the respective religion. While the philosopher sees God as a study of natural reason and related to the total investigation of the nature of the universe, the theologian builds on a philosophy of God and studies how the various Western religions understand this "God" as a revealing agent. The philosopher has the entire natural universe as the arena of his investigation; the theologian looks to the Scriptures of Islam, Christianity or Judaism as the main informational source for her investigation.

The psychological approach is person-centered. Psychology as a scientific study of behavior concerns itself with the origin, development, and maintenance of an individual's religious belief. It says nothing about the truth or validity of a religious system or viewpoint. In contrast to sociology that studies society as a whole, psychology studies the individual person under the category of religion and religious experience.

Phenomena and Phenomenology of Religion

The historian of religion looking to the experiences of foreign and ancient civilizations collects, classifies, and describes the documents that relate this history of the past. Once, however, this scholar attempts to understand these documents or artefacts, or rituals, on their own plane of reference, he enters the discipline of phenomenology.

Like every human phenomenon the religious phenomenon is extremely complex. Each age, each work or symbol, each myth of the age must be studied in itself. As in literature, once the historian of literature has finished his task the literary critic takes over. So also in religion. But when is a literary work finally explained? There is always a hidden message in the work of great writers. In religious works, activities, rituals - as religious phenomena - the historian of religion must bring out the autonomous value of these works. We note however, that religious phenomena are never understood apart from their culture and history. Writing the first important treatise on the subject, G. Van der Leeuw believed the main task of phenomenology of religion is to illumine the inner structures of the religious phenomena.[3] At the center of all religious phenomena is the human person - homo religiosus. Whatever scale we use to measure religious phenomena, it must always adequately measure the chief actor in this religious drama, the human person herself.

Two Disciplines

Eliade believes that in recent years scholars have felt the need to transcend the contrasting disciplines of history of religions and phenomenology of religions to reach a broader perspective that unites these two distinct intellectual operations. Admitting to the inherent tensions of such an understanding Eliade encourages the union of these two disciplines as a creative expression that ultimately stimulates the science of religions. For all practical purposes the historian of religion guides the intellectual activity somewhat like a pilot guides an ocean going freighter into a harbor. The historical endeavor moves through philosophy, psychology, sociology and enters slowly into philosophical and cultural anthropology. Each discipline looks to the religious experience of the person. The religious experiences are viewed as roots for the development of cultures with all their social institutions, art, technology, and ethical ideals. The path is narrow, the passage is slow, but the process brings the ship to rest and to port - all the result of painstaking and skilled direction.

Phenomenology as a Discipline

If history is the pilot, phenomenology is the system and experience of the pilot used for deciding how to bring the ship into port. Among the leading thinkers in the phenomenology of religion are: Mircea Eliade, Ernst Troeltsch, Rudolf Otto, Joachim Wach and Gerardus van der Leeuw. Within that group Joachim Wach typifies the spirit and thrust of the discipline.

For Wach the basic question in the study called phenomenology of religion is "How can I both understand and interpret a religion that I am investigating scientifically?"[4] Admitting to human limitations I must attempt to find what level or grade of understanding I might attain, particularly if the religion under investigation is quite foreign to me. While European centers of learning continued to devote great effort to the study of world religions, Wach looked to American scholarship to enter more openly into the study of Eastern religions and peoples.

There were many difficulties in pursuing the scientific study of religion in America. Strong pietistic trends and equally strong rationalistic reactions to pietism, along with nature mysticism and pragmatism created the danger of developing merely a constructive theology instead of a scientific study. Wach who lost his position in Leipzig in 1935 due to Nazi pressures, relocated himself at Brown University in Rhode Island. After ten years, (1945), he accepted the chair of the History of Religions at Chicago University where he brought zest and vigor to the scientific disciplines. For Wach *Religionswissenschaft** was his life. He considered the science to cover three areas: hermeneutics or the theory of interpretation, the study of religious experience and the sociology of religion. In effect, his *Religionswissenschaft* surveys the nature, characteristics, and functions of religions. When asked if his *Religionswissenschaft* is a theological, philosophical, historical or even social scientific discipline, he replies that it is a *Geisteswissenschaft.*** For Wach, subjective religiousness becomes objectified through expressions and structures that can be comprehended. The study of such structures is primary to the study. In this sense, Wach follows Wilhelm Dilthey's ideas by calling this science a descriptive science.

Wach's descriptive science bases itself on the distinct philosophical tradition that the human person is its central focus. Both philosophy and religion are aware of three basic questions of human life: the nature of ultimate reality, the nature of the universe, and the nature and destiny of the human species. All three are interrelated. All three ask about the basic unity of life. Among the three questions Wach was most intrigued by the third one using anthropology not as a study of human life but as an inquiry into humanity's understanding of itself. Like Luther and Eliade Wach uses the human person as the center of the religious inquiry. Whether we begin with anthropology or move quickly to the study of various societies, we reach out to understand and to interpret religion as a primary activity of the human species. Even in Greece where human values were emphasized more than in any other ancient culture, the basic desire for unity of life was understood in religious categories.

Wach easily recognized that the occidental view of human life with its religions of revelation differed considerably from the oriental view of human life. In the Orient, in Brahman, Buddhist or Taoist thinking, the activity of human living supercedes human identity. Only in Confucianism did Wach find similarities to Greek Western thinking about the conditions of human life. Perhaps his sociological studies pointed out his sincere desire for responsible, clear scientific investigation of religion more than his efforts in other disciplines. Regardless of the given study, Wach brought to our times a sensitivity that present day scholars deeply appreciate as we compare and contrast the effects of religion on individuals and on society.

Focus

The phenomenological approach to religion according to C. G. Jung concerns itself with "occurrences, events, experiences, in a word with facts."[5] Because of its independence as a discipline it serves to produce oftentimes a reconciliation between conflicting methodological approaches of the various disciplines already mentioned. In this book we will focus on the individual person as religious in a social or community setting. As such we will concentrate our attention more upon the sociological, philosophical and psychological approach to religion than upon the other approaches. Naturally, we will anchor our investigation in the idea of religion as a phenomenon that touches every human person and every human culture throughout our limited record of history.

Lest we lose ourselves in the varied disciplines that investigate the chief questions related to religion, I wish to focus on one central issue or question: "How does a contemporary American view religion both as an individual and as part of a community?" Frequently the media remind us that Americans are quite religious, but what does this mean? Moreover, if I practice some sort of religion, how can I review this practice with an eye toward improving my religious attitudes and perhaps shedding the religious trappings of my youth that no longer hold meaning for me. Will I notice in this study that I may be religious as an individual, but may dislike the expression of religion in my community. I ask further: "How does the community support me in my religion?" Would I become arrogant to cease my participation in the local church or community if I felt I retained my basic values in life? These are some of the questions that we will treat in the following chapters.

Because the main issue of this study is rooted in the distinction between individual and community we will approach this material first from a general historical viewpoint (chapter one) of how religion evolves. Before we proceed too far we will attempt a definition or description of religion (chapter two). Then, the two themes of religion - power and holiness - will occupy our attention (chapter three). The material readily leads to a focus on the individual person in the community (chapter four) and how this person responds psychologically (chapter five). In the last two chapters (chapters six and seven) we will concentrate more forcefully on the experience of religion in one's life and how one makes choices ultimately to express her or his religion authentically. At all times we return to the main issue: each person, as person, is both individual and communal. How this affects the person's attitude toward religion becomes central to our focus.

Discussion Questions

1) Discuss the several approaches available to the study of religion based on existing disciplines.

2) Contrast the theological and philosophical approach to religion.

3) Describe the distinctive traits distinguishing the history of religion from the phenomenology of religion.

Notes

* The science of religion

** The study of the Humanities

1 Mircea Eliade, *Pattern of Comparative Religion* (New York: Meridian Books, The World Publishing Co., 1958), p. 3ff.

2 For a more detailed treatment of the role of anthropology in solving religious issues cf. Geoffrey E. W. Scobie, *Psychology of Religion* (London: B. T. Batsford Ltd., 1973), pp. 16-18.

3 Mircea Eliade, *The Quest* (Chicago: The University of Chicago Press, 1959), p. 35ff.

4 Joseph M. Kitagawa, "Introduction: The Life and Thought of Joachim Wach," *The Comparative Study of Religion*, Joachim Wach, (New York: Columbia University Press, 1958), p. xxiii.

5 Carl Gustav Jung, *Psychology and Religion* (New Haven: Yale University Press, 1977), p. 3.

Chapter One

The Evolution of Religion

Proceeding from Clifford Geertz's[1] definition of religion, Robert Bellah reflects on the evolution of religion in the limited sense that religion is a set of symbolic forms and acts that relate persons to the ultimate condition of their existence.[2] For Bellah, it is not the ultimate conditions that have evolved, nor the human person's situation. What has evolved is religion itself as a symbol system. The human person indeed has evolved from primitive to modern times, but whether primitive or modern the human person is fully a religious person at any stage of his existence. What truly evolves is this religious person's complex set of relationships and symbols that convert him to his ultimate conditions in life. While there are many ways to assess religious evolution Bellah concentrates on this development within a theoretical formulation of five stages: primitive, archaic, historic, early modern, and modern. Distinguished temporally in the most general sense these stages allow us to see the development of religious activity throughout our cultural systems.

Primitive Religion

Before we consider the elements of primitive religion, let us look at two background elements affecting human religious history:

1) By 1000 B.C. in the centers of high culture, there was an overwhelming rejection of the world resulting in a negative evolution of human life and the exaltation of another reality as infinitely valuable. Developing from Plato's classic formulation in *Phaedo* that the body is the prison of the soul, and

that the soul yearns to unite with the divine life by freeing itself from this prison, we find a most radical version of Pla-
tonic world rejection in the Buddhist conviction that the
world is a burning house and each of us needs a way to escape
from it. In China Taoist ascetics urged a transvaluation of accepted worldly values and encouraged withdrawal from human society. The *Koran* recommends life to come as infinitely superior to the present life. In Japan Shotoku Thishi
declared that the world is a lie, and only Buddhas is true. In
the Kamakura period the conviction that the world is hell led
to orgies of religious suicide by those seeking Amida's par-
adise. We have comparable sentiments in Christianity in
Pauline and Augustinian theology. Although these rejections
of the world showed variations after 1000 B.C. there were
many examples of this world rejection in religious history.

2)   By contrast, there is a virtual absence of world rejection in
primitive religions. Primitive religions look at reality as a single cosmos. They do not look to another world as better than
the present one, or as some sort of end goal or "salvation" after living in this present world. The religious person in primitive times looked to religion as the maintenance of cosmic
harmony by seeking to enjoy human gifts and benefits such as
health, good crops, happy family life, as values suitable for religious acceptance. While an idea of salvation outside the
present world dominates world rejecting religion, primitive
religion sees cosmic harmony as "salvation" in the present
world. After death, life consists of a shadowy, ill defined existence in the hands of the "gods." Because there is little world
rejection in our theology today, we have come to appreciate
more deeply the attitude of the primitive religious person.

   Lucien Levy-Bruhl characterizes the primitive religious symbol
system as "the mythical world".[3] W. E. H. Stanner as a most bril-

liant interpreter of Australian religion confirms Levy-Bruhl's position by translating this mythical world as "the dreaming," or time out of time, or an "everywhen" world inhabited by ancestral figures, some human, some divine. Though these ancestral figures take on heroic proportions, and are by reputation metahuman, they are not gods and they do not control the world and consequently are not worshipped.

In primitive religion the participant seeks to identify himself to the extent of relating the actual world to the mythical world. Each clan and each local group became identified with their ancestors and past events. Virtually all reality, every mountain, tree, and rock is explained in terms of the actions of mythical beings. All human action is prefigured in the Dreaming, both folly and crimes, virtue and vice; all present actual existence and the ancestral myths as intimately as humanly possible.

At the primitive level religious organization is not separated from the social structure. Church and society are one. Religious roles are fused with other public and personal roles, and differentiation in terms of age, sex, and kinship groups are distinctly important. Leadership comes to certain male age groups. Clans receive the ceremonial traditions based on ancestry. Ritual is the main primitive religious action, not as sacrifice but as a means to identify with the mythical beings the primitive participants represent. Because primitive life is fluid and flexible it successfully avoids radical innovation.

In sum, the primitive symbol system is myth and the religious action is ritual. The mythical beings are not addressed or beseeched as a worship exercise, but the participant seeks to be identified with the mythical being to such an extent that the distance between the mythical being and the human participant becomes slight and may even disappear in the power of the ritual experience itself. With no priests, or congregations, all present in the ritual become involved in the ritual action and the identification with the myth itself.

Archaic Religion

By restricting the concept of primitive religion to Australia, Bellah correspondingly relates archaic religion to the religious systems of much of Africa, Polynesia, the ancient Middle East, India and China. The distinguishing feature of archaic religion is the emergence of cult with the complexity of gods, priests, worship and sacrifice. The ritual and myth of primitive religion develops and is systematized within the structure of archaic religion.

In archaic religion the mythical beings become objectified and thought of as controlling the natural world including human life. These beings have become "gods," and as such are respected according to hierarchies of control. All things, both divine and natural in this world have a place. A vast and sometimes detailed cosmology emerges. The symbol systems now become more stable under the care of priestly types. The division between persons and gods becomes clearer, and more delineated. The need for communication between the two grows. Worship and sacrifice and priestly mediation take on a new value. Hence human persons look to the ultimate conditions of their existence with more awareness, more freedom, but with an increased burden of anxiety. As the social structures of archaic religion proliferate, cults multiply and a two-class system emerges. The upper class dominates military and political life and tends to control religious life as well. Noble families provide kings and assume special priestly functions as well. Specialized priesthoods may develop at cult centers but the political elite never divests itself of religious leadership. Unfortunately the cult centers show one limitation of archaic religion by failing to develop a laity or "faithful" to join with the organized priesthood. Meanwhile the individual and his social grouping become merged in a descriptive natural-divine cosmos. The practice of religion for any religious adherent, priest or layperson, is grounded in this divinely instituted cosmic order.

Historic Religion

This stage in Bellah's theoretical scheme is called historic because: a) the religions included are relatively recent falling chiefly under the discipline of history rather than archeology or ethnography, and b) they are all in some sense transcendental. Hence, world rejection at this stage for the first time becomes a general characteristic of a religious system, and as transcendental, the symbol systems are all dualistic.

Admitting the variety of symbol systems in historic religion, they all stress an hierarchical ordering both in the supernatural realm above and in the world we inhabit. For the average believer this new dualism manifests itself in a belief in a life after death infinitely superior or with the emergence of various ideas of hell, infinitely worse than our present world.

Belief in the after-life gives way to the religious goal of salvation (enlightenment, or release, etc.) as the chief religious preoccupation. Relying on elements of archaic cosmology, the identity of the individual believer is no longer tied to his individual clan or tribe but moves out into the world and can be related to the transcendental goals and expressions of the universe. In historical religion, religious activities are needed for salvation. Ritual and sacrifice now take on new meanings as stress on the flawed character of each human calls for serious action in the believer's religious life. According to Buddhism, for example, each person's nature is described as greed and anger. In Islam, the believer must submit to the will of God. For the first time, the individual puts together a structured conception of the self in the light of a devalued empirical world and a diffused universal reality. The self is seen as deeper than the flux of everyday reality. While primitive persons can only accept the world in its manifest givenness, and archaic persons fulfill religious obligations and attain peace with the gods through sacrifice, historic religions promise humans for the first time that they can understand the basic structure of reality and through salvation, actively participate in it.

This striving for salvation sets the devout apart from the rest of the world, and ideally the special believers withdraw from the world. The single religio-political hierarchy of archaic society now splits into two partially, at least, independent hierarchies - one political, one religious. Now political power and religious power must be shared, and the masses assume the distinction between believer and subject. More classes emerge and literacy and the market-economy supports a greater sharing of power. In fact, religious innovation arises from the broad urban middle class. Religion now provides the idealogy and social cohesion for many tensions and rebellions among the empowered leaders allowing for more dynamic and purposive social change.

Early Modern Religion

The defining characteristic of early modern religion is the collapse of the hierarchical structure of both this and the other world. While dualism remains, there is more direct confrontation between the two worlds. Under early modern conceptions salvation is not found by withdrawing from the world, but by actively involving oneself in the world. No longer do monks and special religious leaders hold priviledged status, as mediators of salvation. With the Reformation the entire mediated system of salvation through religious leaders is dropped and in its place salvation is made available directly to any person regardless of station or calling. While reform movements occurred in all major religions, the Protestant Reformation is the only attempt that was successfully institutionalized. As early modern religion develops the dualism remains, but the Reformation reinforced positive autonomous action in the world instead of relatively passive acceptance of the world. Religious action more and more is viewed as identical with the whole of life. Special devotional practices are dropped, and faith as an internal equality is highlighted. Salvation now is recognized as coming in spite of sin, not in its absolute absence. Religion in its social organization becomes based more on contract and voluntary association, than on paternalistic authority.

Modern Religion

The central feature of modern religion, found already in the early modern category of Bellah, is the collapse of the dualism so crucial to all historical religion. The first trace of the fundamental break with traditional historical symbol systems comes in the work of Kant. His ethical grounding of religion points decisively in the direction of modern religious development. With the advances of the past two centuries, hierarchic dualistic religious symbol systems fall away and yield to a multiplex symbol system rooted in the complex situation of human life today. Friedrich Schleiermacher is the key figure in nineteenth century Western theology that becomes involved in finding new symbols to express religious living. By the twentieth century, Tillich, Bultmann, Bonhoeffer and others set the stage for a radical reappraisal of doctrines, worship and religious life-styles. Based on the definition of religion as the symbolization of human relations to the ultimate conditions of existence, no one church or group can claim to control religious development. Modern religion applies the development of psychology to religious traditions and helps contemporary religious persons take responsibility for their own fate.

Today, less than ever will our search for meaning be confined to institutional religion. With the collapse of clearly defined doctrines, or an objective system of moral standards, religious action in the world will be more demanding than ever. The search for adequate standards of action becomes at the same time a search for personal maturity and social relevance. These actions coalesce into our modern search for salvation not as a dualistic other-worldly experience but as a socially and personally alert sense of the ultimate value of our existence.

Conclusion

This theoretical division of religious evolution is based on the proposition that at each stage freedom of personality and society has increased relative to the current conditions of human existence. In time human existence becomes more complex, more open to change and development. Social evolution, if accepted as normal to human evolutionary growth, implies religious evolution as well. The self must grow and become identified. Meanwhile society grows and each person develops a sharper sense of relatedness to the social world - ever moving, ever becoming more clearly perceived. To learn of self and of the world creates tensions with rejection of one in favor of concentration on the other until both take their place in a more understandable universalized scheme of accord and appreciation.

Discussion Questions

Chapter One

1) What elements of primitive religion do we find in our contemporary culture?

2) Discuss how reasonable it appears for two classes to emerge from archaic religion.

3) Discuss the general characteristics of historical religion, and its contrast with early modern and modern religion.

Notes

1 Clifford Geertz, "Religion as a Cultural System" in Michael Banton, ed., *Anthropological Approaches to The Study of Religion*, A. S. A. Monographs, vol. 3 (London: Tavistock Press, 1966) p. 4.

2 Robert Bellah, *Beyond Belief* (New York: Harper and Row, Publishers, 1970), pp. 21-30.

3 *Ibid.*, p. 26.

Chapter Two

What is Religion?

In approaching this question we ask immediately to whose realm belongs the study of religion. Already we admit the sociologist and psychologist has a vested interest, but is it properly more in the scope of the philosopher or the theologian? Or, in other words, what is the difference between the philosopher of religion and the theologian? Basically, the philosopher is differentiated from the theologian by the method that each employs in looking at fixed beliefs. The philosophy of religion has been conceived as a subdivision of philosophy that deals with uniquely religious aspects of reality, knowledge and values relying exclusively on the use of human intelligence. The theologian relies ultimately on a faith response to a supposed revelation or revelatory event in arriving at his understanding of the uniquely religious features of reality, knowledge, and value. Thus, revelation is the difference. The philosopher and related to him, the sociologist, and psychologist, rely on the full force of human powers of intelligence. Beyond this the theologian accepts the fact and content of revelation from "God" or a divine being as informative of the religious features of reality.

Ideally the philosopher of religion develops a systematic elaboration of what human intelligence can discover all by itself about such religious issues as the existence and characteristics of God, the problem of evil, the relation of man to God, destiny and meaning.

Keeping this distinction in mind we return again to the question, what is religion? Openly we must admit that this is one of the most difficult questions to answer in the total academic study of the subject. Because religion is such a broad topic, the very attempt to put limits on the term is taxing. Definitions are attempted for various reasons. For example, they serve:

1)   to report the meaning attached to various words.

2)   to find the limits of the topic.

3)   to connect the symbols with the common understanding of the symbols.

Rem Edwards[1] in looking into the definitions of religion calls for two steps before attempting a persuasive definition.

1)   search for a common essence

2)   search for family resemblances

The Search for a Common Essence

Immediately we ask what property or set of characteristics must a thing have before we call it religious or religion. What is singularly essential to religion? The attempt to find the common essence of religion is not so easy as it seems. For example, if we say that religion is "belief in God," we are confronted by the fact that many of the great world religions such as early Buddhism, Zen Buddhism, and Hinayana Buddhism that prevail today in Southeast Asia are completely atheistic. Or, if we say religion is a belief in the supernatural we are confronted with the fact that many versions of pantheism such as those developed by the Stoics and Spinoza, tend to identify God with nature and allow no place at all for the supernatural. Furthermore, religion in process theology tends to break down any distinction between the natural and the supernatural. The search for the common essence of religion is complicated further by the fact that humanism has become a "religion" for some people as Communism and Marxism have for others, but whereas these may provide answers to the questions of the meaning of life or the meaning of history, neither makes a place for such traditional religious concerns as the supernatural or life after death. Moreover, we often hear of some acquaintance who is said to have made a "religion" out of wealth, or success, or golf. Do these values have anything in common with the traditional world religions? What is the common essence of religion?

Tillich's Definition of Religion

We must admit from the outset that the result of any attempt to find a factor common to such diverse ideas as Christianity, Communism and golf must necessarily be extremely diffuse, diluted and abstract. Paul Tillich has made such a definition providing at least a common denominator for religion. He states:

> Religion is the state of being grasped by an ultimate concern, a concern which qualifies all other concerns as preliminary and which itself contains the answer to the question of the meaning of our life.[2]

Both the great and small religions of the world seem to qualify, for the people who belong to them find themselves grasped by the ultimate concern. They find themselves in possession of a value or values that give meaning and unity to the whole of their lives and to which all other values are subordinate.

Ultimate as Pivotal

Tillich uses the adjective ultimate to modify the word concern but sometimes he applies it to the object of that concern, so that religion seems to mean an ultimate concern about an ultimate object. As he further unfolds this definition this essential characteristic of religion resides not in the religious beliefs or objects, but in the human response to them. There is no attempt to find a common belief or object in religion. The common essence of religion lies in man's response to these objects. Thus he allows for a wide variety of religions, but provides a common characteristic to distinguish an act of man as truly religious.

Idolatry

Tillich considers idolatry as a concern about that which is not truly ultimate in itself. In true faith the ultimate concern is about the truly ultimate; while in idolatrous faith preliminary concerns are elevated to the rank of ultimate concern. Here of course, we find a judgment on Tillich's part about the objectivity of ultimacy. Tillich states his case against idolatry so strongly that he sometimes conveys the impression that an ultimate concern about a less-than-ultimate object would not really count as a "religion" at all. Furthermore, ultimate suggests singularity. Hence, no polytheistic religions would qualify. Ultimate becomes a term loaded in favor of monism and monotheism. Thus the more Tillich interprets the term ultimate the more narrow and less characteristic it becomes for a description of world religion. Perhaps, Tillich does not want to deny that idolatrous religion is religion, but his judgments appear to be quite fixed against idolatrous examples. Nevertheless, since both have ultimate concern in common, they are religions in the mind of the subject who regards them as ultimate.

Ultimate – Is it a Proper Word?

Because the word ultimate in its normal meaning applies only to the last member of a series, and because it appears that a man who has an ultimate concern is a well integrated individual it appears that the word ultimate does not admit of degrees in the act of religion. Without a conception of degrees of religiosity we are faced with the conclusion that a not-so-well integrated church goer whose religious life is less intense than that of the great "saints" cannot be considered a religious person. Would it not be better to substitute for the word ultimate INTENSE, so that religion could admit of various degrees of concern in the average religious person? Could we not rather say religion is the state of "being grasped by an intense concern," which provides sufficient meaning for life. Again we must admit that in striving for the widest possible definition of religion we perhaps dilute the idea of religion to the point where we must ask for more specification in the notion of religion. Although "ultimate concern" seems to be common to all religions, it does not distinguish them adequately. So, we look further for more concrete details from these accepted phrases – "ultimate concern" or intense concern. In order to accomplish this we move to a search of family resemblances in religion.

FAMILY TRAITS	Success, Wealth Golf, Fishing, etc.	Spinozistic Pantheism	Moral Naturalistic Humanism	Communism	Aristotle's Concept of Unmoved Mover	Early Greek Olympian Polytheism	Early Buddhism and Hinayana Buddhism	Vedanta Hindu Pantheism	Christianity, Judaism, Islam
1. Belief in a supernatural intelligent being or beings	A	A	A	A	P	A	A	A?	P
2. Belief in superior intelligent being or beings	A	A?	A	A	P	P	A	P	P
3. Complex world view interpreting the significance of human	A	P	P	P	P	P	P	P	P
4. Belief in experience after death	A	A	A	A	A	P?	P	P	P
5. Moral code	A	A	P	P	P	A	P	P	P
6. Belief that the moral code is sanctioned by a superior intelligent being or beings	A	A	A	A	A	A	A	P	P
7. An account of the nature of, origin of, and cure for evil	A	P	P	P	P	P?	P	P	P
8. Theodicy	A	A	A	A	A	A	A	P?	P
9. Prayer and ritual	A	A?	A	P?	A	P	P	P	P
10. Sacred objects and places	A?	A	A	P	A	P	P	P	P
11. Revealed truths or interpretations of revelatory events	A	A	A	A	A	P	P?	P	P
12. Religious experience - awe, mystical experience, revelations	P	A	A	A	A	P	P	P	P
13. Deep, intense concern	P	P	P	P	P?	P	P	P	P
14. Institutionalized social sharing of some of traits 1-13	A?	A?	A?	P	A?	P	P	P	P

Key: P = Present, A = Absent, ? = Unclear.

Courtesy of Rem Edwards.

The Search for Family Resemblances

Ludwig Wittgenstein tells us that there are many meaningful useful words in our language that have no "common essence" of connotation. He believes that it is not always possible to find the common essence of a term. For example, he lists such words as: game, language, knowledge, art and play. Rather than look to a common essence for every use of this type of word we might more effectively explore the family traits of a term in order to understand the nature and application of the term. Just as members of a family resemble one another but do not necessarily share in one common trait, we still can find out much about the family. If we pursue the study of religion in the same way, we might broaden our understanding of the term without demanding that one or more common traits pervade all religions. On the preceding page is a chart showing 14 family traits of various religions of East and West.[3] Across the top of the page are listed nine categories of the chief "religions" of our experience.

The first category is Christianity, Judaism and Islam. In this category each religion has a common understanding of God as the object of religion and a factor in each person's salvation or attainment of heaven. The second category is Vedanta Hindu and pantheism. For the pantheist all is god and many interpretations of Hinduism are pantheistic in this sense. In Hinduism the forces of nature - the sea, earth and sky - are represented by a host of gods. As such polytheism prevails, but certain gods are more prominent. Throughout this category individual man attempts to be at peace with the forces of nature which often are the same as god.

The third category is Early Buddhism and Hinayana Buddhism. In this grouping the Buddhist denies belief in any god who might influence a person's life. There are deities who live in heavenly spheres, but no god is important in the plan of salvation; no outside power can come to the aid of humankind. The fourth category is Early Greek Olympian Polytheism. In this grouping the gods are not considered to be beyond nature or prior to nature. These gods are not creators of nature, but were created out of the original chaos of nature itself. They are personifications of such natural entities as darkness, light, earth, heaven, time and the planets.

The fifth category is the concept of Unmoved Mover in Aristotle. This Unmoved Mover is beyond the spatial order of everyday events. Nature depends on this Unmoved Mover for its motion in a way that an effect depends on a cause. To Aristotle, this Mover is not beyond time, because the world of nature coexists with the Unmoved Mover throughout an infinite past.

The sixth category is Communism. We will regard this category as one political, economic and sociological version of naturalistic humanism. In Communism, the object is to change the world order to provide for the ultimate dignity of the human species. Communism finds the value of human life in the pursuit and attainment of the equality of possession, opportunity for human expression and happiness. At this juncture we need not enter into a discussion of the Russian, Chinese, or other national versions of Communism.

The seventh category is Moral Naturalistic Humanism. In this category the world of nature constitutes the sum total of reality. Nature needs no explanation for us, the creatures of nature, but in nature all legitimate explanations of reality take place. Sometimes nature is a friend to mankind; sometimes it is his foe. Regardless, human persons should pursue and achieve whatever ideal goals they can attain such as: beauty, truth, goodness and scientific productivity. In this humanism espoused by John Dewey and by many of his contemporaries, supernaturalism has no reality.

The eighth category is Spinozistic Pantheism. For Spinoza, God and nature are identical, and more powerful than individual persons or corporate mankind. Spinoza does not define God or nature as distinctly intelligent, but rather they comprise the sum total of all finite human intelligence. God is not so much in charge of the world as "he" is a part of everything in the world.

The final and ninth category is: success, wealth, golf etc. In this group belong those people who see these distinct achievements as the reality of religion. This group pursues a goal that may seem ultimate to them, but according to outside observers appears to be less than ultimate and limited in religious value.

In reviewing the family traits of these nine categories we might move quickly to confront our misconceptions about religion and religions other than the one we follow. For example, many college students who enroll in a world religions course believe that in all religions some sort of a "god" is worshipped, one that is comparable to the supernatural deity of Western religions. Furthermore, many students believe that all world religions include a moral or ethical code somewhat like the Ten Commandments of Judaism.

By investigating the following family traits we not only identify specific religions but by relating characteristics of one religion to another we develop a "sense" of religion without demanding a common essential characteristic to be understood in our description of religion. While the following list of family traits of religions is hardly complete it does give a ready practical means of distinguishing the various religions accepted in our world today.

1. Belief in a Supernatural Intelligent Being or Beings

The key word here is supernatural, i.e. beyond nature, or beyond the realm of spatiotemporal reality of our every day experience which is the primary subject of scientific investigation. The God of Judaism, Islamism, and Christianity is clearly a supernatural being who is thought to have existed before time and before the world of nature came into being. Aristotle's philosophical concept of unmoved mover sees God as beyond space but not time. Thus his supernatural role is somewhat limited. However, in the other major religions the notion of God is not tied to a totally supernatural being in the way in which the God of the chief Western religions is regarded.

2. Belief in a Superior Intelligent Being or Beings

Superior divinities may enjoy immense powers, but unlike supernatural divinities, are not necessarily beyond the spatiotemporal universe. The clearest example is found in Greek Olympian polytheism where the gods are accepted as part of nature although they are endowed with immense powers. Note the interrogative point in the category of Spinozistic pantheism. For Spinoza, God and nature are identical and infinitely more powerful than man. The problem lay in determining whether or not Spinoza's God is intelligent power. Notice the number of categories clearly lacking a belief in a superior intelligent being.

3. **Complex World View Interpreting the Significance of Human Life**

Christians find their questions about the meaning and destiny of human life answered in the complex drama of Creation, Fall, Incarnation, Atonement, Kingdom of God, Death, Final Judgment, Heaven and Hell. All the other major religions likewise provide some interpretation for the significance of human life. In this sense it is one of the two or three characteristics found in all religions. One distinctive explanation is that of naturalistic humanism. This "religion" holds: that the world of nature constitutes the sum total of reality, that nature does not have to be explained but provides the context within which all legitimate explanations take place, that it has always existed and that sometimes it is friendly to man and sometimes not. Man's purpose is to pursue and attain whatever ideal ends he sets for himself such as the value of human associations, artistic creativity or any other goals that may arise from his natural interests and activities.

4. **Belief in Experience After Death**

While it is common for us as Westerners (especially Christian and Islamic) to assume that religion indicates the continuation of individual experience after death there are some religions that fail to do this. Hinduism and Hinayana Buddhism assure their adherents that experience after death is not a permanent condition and that it is not desirable. The cycle of reincarnation need not endure forever, in fact, a means of escape from the wheel of rebirth is often sought in these Oriental religions. The New Testament confrontation of the question of the resurrection among the Pharisees and Saducees is indicative of the division that exists in Western thought. The dismal Greek view of life after death exemplified in that writing of Homer provides macabre material for contemporary horror stories. In general, the more modern the movement towards contemporary humanism, the less emphasis is placed on life after death.

5. Moral Code

Not every code of conduct in a religious system of values is a moral one. In describing a moral code as that which is designed to promote the welfare of humanity as a whole, we find that some religions fail to incorporate a moral point of view. (Note the dominance of adherence to moral codes shown in the chart.)

6. Belief that a Moral Code is Sanctioned By a Superior Intelligent Being

Ivan Karomazov says: "If God does not exist, then anything is permitted."[4] A brief glance at the chart will show that this idea is not shared by most world religions. While it is true of most Western religions, it is not true of Hinayana Buddhism for the simple reason that there are no divinities. It is also not true of humanism, and communism, for the same reason. For both Aristotle and Spinoza there is little logical connection between human values and divine will.

7. An Account of Evil

As the chart shows the attempt to deal with the nature, origins and cure for evil is nearly a universal trait of religion, but the theories proposed differ significantly from religion to religion. Distinguishing natural evil (flood, storms, deformity etc.) from moral evil (caused by rational beings as moral agents), most religions agree that there are both types of evil in the world. Western theistic religion emphasizes the role of moral disobedience in introducing pain and suffering into the world. Traditionally, up to recent years, they hold there was no evil before the "Fall." Both Hinduism and Buddhism also see evil as originating to some extent in immortality. The ancient Greeks saw evil as emerging along with good from the life of the gods. Although major religions hold out the hope that evil can be cured, they differ drastically in their interpretation of how this is to be effected. Christians and Jews see a cure in a responsible relationship of man to God in a life of grace. Hindus and Buddhists look to salvation as the loss of the finite self and the ultimate release from the wheel of rebirth. Unlike the naturalistic humanists who despair of an ultimate cure for evil, the Communists see this cure in the political evolution of a classless society.

8. Theodicy

Over and above the general issue of evil theodicy is the attempt to reconcile belief in the goodness and power of God with the fact of evil in the world. Theodicy is peculiar to the monotheistic religions that attribute moral perfection and immense power to God. Other religions do not demand an explanation of how good and evil exist in a meaning system.

9. Prayer and Ritual

Prayer and ritual are found in most of the major world religions and in early Greek religion. Spinoza bridges the gap between traditional theistic views about prayer and humanistic denial of a need for prayer. Spinoza allowed a kind of prayer of meditation in his notion of the intellectual love of God but allowed no place for prayers of intercession or ritual worship. Ritual strangely enough seems most elaborately developed today in High Church Christianity.

10. Sacred Objects and Places

Most of the major world religions hold sacred places and sacred objects in veneration. Even the Communists in Russia cherish references to their leaders (e.g. Lenin's tomb).

11. Revealed Truths

Most of the great world religions have a fund of revelation that is usually incorporated in sacred scriptures such as: The Old and New Testament, Koran, Vedas, Upanishads. With the possible exception of Buddhism, revelation is missing both in the atheistic religions such as Communism and humanism, and those theistic religions based on natural philosophical intelligence (Aristotle, Spinoza).

12. Religious Experience

Religious experience is present in most of the great world religions, however, it does not follow that each sincere devotee of one of these religions receives personal revelation or enters states of mystical ecstacy.

13. Deep Intense Concern

Linked to Tillich's idea of "ultimate concern" in religion we see this as one of the most common characteristics of religion. This category raises the question of how much personal involvement must occur before you have a religion. The more philosophical we are about religion the less involvement seems to be required.

Institutionalized Sharing of Some Traits 1 Through 13

We now ask: "can there be a purely private religion?" A. N. Whitehead defines religion as "What a man does with his own solitariness,"[5] but many sociologists such as Wach, Durkheim and Yinger insist that religion is essentially a social phenomenon. According to our chart there are ample indications of shared traits. But we must further distinguish social sharing and permanent institutions. In general we can say social sharing is rather typical and widespread, at least in five categories.

Conclusions

The only family members that exhibit all the traits listed are the Western religions. This suggests that these religions have a great influence on our conception of religion in general. Should we have set it up to arrive at a "P" for the oriental religions, some of the Western religions would not qualify under the selected traits. More than just the number of family traits, the importance of these traits assist us in accounting for an overall view of religion. For Westerners belief in God and in experience after death, the problem of evil and intense concern seem to weigh heavily on our scales of assessment. How strange it is that a Western atheist, who denies God and immortality, never prays, and who holds to principles that we in our area consider less than moral, would not be called by us a religious person, but a dedicated Hinayana Buddhist who fails to affirm God and immortality, yet engages in some form of prayer and holds to some system of morality is considered a religious person, mainly because his system exhibits a significant number of important characteristics on our chart.

Thus we have different traits to assist us in our progress toward an understanding of what religion is. We now can operate more comfortably without a precise definition, and while these traits gain acceptance without being placed as absolute conditions, the variety and flexibility implied in the term religion remains.

A Definition of Religion

Charles Stevenson suggests that some definitions are meant to persuade people.[6] This is often displayed by introducing the definition with such words as true or real. For example, if someone wishes to define true love or the real meaning of freedom, we should be prepared for a definition intended to influence our attitudes or values. The word religion, because it traditionally evokes in us a serious or warm response, lends itself readily to a persuasive definition. To illustrate this further we will review the persuasive definitions of Kant and Schleiermacher. Of course, before we start we must admit that a definition will list traits which by their isolation suggest singular importance to the exclusion of other traits. Always the one who defines religion presumes that his own view of religion should be universally accepted and is in a superior position in terms of other religions.

Kant defines religion as: "the recognition of all duties as divine commands."[7] Note how his definition is tied to an ethical or duty bound concept of life. In effect religion is reduced to moral living; everything else is non-essential. Kant insisted that first we discover morality and from this we derive our conception of God. He sees morality in terms of the transcendent life of man that continues after death in the reception of immortality enjoyed in proportion to his moral life on earth. Dismissing revelation Kant understands the whole notion of God as derivative from a knowledge of morality.

By general consensus among scholars Schleiermacher was one of the greatest theologians of the nineteenth century. From his pietistic background he came to view religion as rooted in individual piety and religious experience. He was particularly anxious to deliver religion from two misconceptions: doctrinalism and moralism. However, while doctrinalism and moralism have no integral role in religion, we are not committed to saying that they play no role whatsoever. For Schleiermacher religion is: "a feeling of absolute dependence." Religion for Schleiermacher is an affection, a revelation of the Infinite God in finite man.

In the last analysis, these two persuasive definitions of religion reduce religion to morality or feeling, thereby eliminating many other acceptable characteristics that the common religious person of today regards as valid and acceptable. At this point we may feel somewhat cool towards any precise definition of the subject of our investigation. But we should move forward and review at least some of the more recent definitions of religion.

Towards a Definition Today

J. Milton Yinger offers a contemporary description of religion. He says:

> Religion is the attempt to "relativize" the individual's desires, as well as his fears, by subordinating them to the conception of absolute good more in harmony with the shared and often mutually contradictory needs and desires of human groups. Certain kinds of belief and action very commonly, if not universally, develop from this double root of religion — the fundamental individual and group needs.[8]

This sensitive contrast between individual religious man and the community is seen in another light by Wm. James' definition of religion. Admitting it to scrutiny as an arbitrary definition he says that religion is:

> The feelings, acts and experiences of individual men in their solitude, so far as they apprehend themselves to stand in relation to whatever they may consider the divine.[9]

Somewhat close to this definition, A. N. Whitehead defines religion as "what man does with his own solitariness."[10] Furthermore Gerard Lenski more sensitive to the relation of communal and individual religiosity defines religion as:

> a system of beliefs about the nature of the forces ultimately shaping a man's destiny, and the practices associated therewith, shared by the members of a group.[11]

Eugene Fontinell describes religion as:

> a phenomenon which involves beliefs, ideas, symbols, practices, institutions distinguishable from other phenomena, such as art, science and politics.[12]

From the above description (definition) we find that religion is important only if it adds a dimension to human life which would be absent without it. The pragmatists latch on to that idea insisting that religion be seen "ultimately" as useful and not simply in the ethereal dreams of an ivory tower romanticist.

Robert Mellert reminds us that process theology prompts us to start with religion not God. As we grow in the world we experience the religious along with the secular to the point where we begin to grasp the truth that there is more at issue in the world than meets the eye. Eventually in Western experience a sense of the reality of God develops and becomes intuited from reality as a whole. Thus man is first religious and only secondarily a believer. "Religion," says Mellert, "is not a consequence of his believing, but a condition for it."[13] After we begin to respond to personal and communal needs that deal with the ultimate questions in life, we begin to specify what we believe in. For Jews, the belief in the personal God of Abraham, Isaac and Jacob sets them apart as distinct believers, believers in a God who speaks in some way to them. For Christians, this God reveals himself finally in His Son Jesus. The Christian moves beyond ordinary religion to a particular belief as a response to this God of Jesus Christ speaking to him. This response is Christian faith.

Rudolph Bultmann was once asked, "What is the difference between the God of philosophy and the God of religion?" He replied: "The God of philosophy is anyone's God, the God of religion is your God and mine."[14] We might add the God of Jews and Christians is a God who speaks and invites a response which technically we call faith.

Because of our human condition we can appreciate Yinger's and Lenski's idea that the double root of religion is our basic individual and group needs. From these two definitions and in comparison with the other definitions that support Yinger and Lenski, we begin our study of religion.

Study Outline

What is Religion?

a) Search For Common Essence

- Many Problems

- Man's Response to Religion as Only Common Essence

b) Search For Family Resemblances

c) Tillich's Idea of Ultimate Concern

- Problem

- Does Religion Admit Degrees of Intensity Moving Toward Ultimate but Not Yet Ultimate For Some Persons?

- Could we Change Ultimate to Intense?

d) Some Definitions

Discussion Questions

Chapter Two

1. Why must we admit there is a problem in trying to define religion?

2. Discuss Tillich's definition of religion. What are its strengths and weaknesses?

3. What are three or four family traits of religion that are shared by most religions?

Notes

1 Rem B. Edwards, *Reason and Religion* (New York: Harcourt Brace Jovanovich, Inc., 1972), p. 6.

2 Paul Tillich, *Christianity and the Encounter of World Religions* (New York: Columbia University Press, 1964), p. 4.

3 Rem B. Edwards, *op. cit.*, pp. 16, 17.

4 *Ibid.*, quoted on p. 26.

5 Alfred North Whitehead, *Religion In The Making* (New York: The New American Library, Inc., Meridian Book, 1960), p. 16.

6 Rem B. Edwards, *op. cit.*, p. 42.

7 Immanuel Kant, *Religion Within the Limits of Reason Alone* (LaSalle, Ill.: Open Court, 1934), p. 142.

8 J. Milton Yinger, *Religion, Society and the Individual* (New York: The MacMillan Co., 1957), p. 16.

9 William James, *The Varieties of Religious Experience* (New York: The New American Library, Inc., A Mentor Book, 1958), p. 42.

10 Alfred North Whitehead, *op. cit.*, p. 16.

11 Gerard Lenski, *The Religious Factor* (Garden City, N.Y.: Doubleday & Co., 1961), p. 331.

12 Eugene Fontinell, *Towards a Reconstruction of Religion* (Garden City, N.Y.: Doubleday & Co., 1970), p. 212.

13 Robert Mellert, *What Is Process Theology?* (New York: The Paulist Press, 1975), p. 37.

14 Quoted in: Charles Hartshorne, *A Natural Theology for Our Time* (LaSalle, Ill.: Open Court Press, 1964), p. 132.

Chapter Three

Power, The Eruption of Holiness

Introduction

Whether you talk to main-line Christian believers, Buddhists, members of sects, or to the so-called "unchurched," almost everyone will agree that religion generates two sharp ideas: power and holiness. Most people are impressed by the power that operates in the historical expression of religion, and most are likewise impressed by the holiness that attracts the interest of the typical believer in religion.

As a child growing up in mid-town, middle class Milwaukee, a town well characterized as middle America, I was impressed by the central position of religion in our neighborhood. When I returned to my neighborhood twenty years later, I noticed a great amount of change, briefly described as urban renewal. Almost all of the buildings in my old neighborhood were torn down and replaced by fresh sparkling new homes. But, midst all this change, the local parish church, St. Michael's, stood more bold than ever before. My parish church was without doubt the largest, the most beautiful, the most dramatic piece of architecture in the neighborhood. The power of religion here spoke eloquently in the sturdy Gothic structure of crafted white block pieced together almost a century ago. I saw in that church also a symbol for the holiness of God reaching heavenward in Gothic majesty all the while reminding me of its counterpart - power.

As I grew up, the idea of God was the most holy, the most powerful idea I knew. Until I read Rudolf Otto's The *Idea of the Holy* I did not understand precisely why the holiness of God was so tremendous, so fascinating, and so compelling a mystery. Eventually I came to understand that this sanctity of God was a link to the power of God the world described at that time. Eventually I developed some tentative, if not much mulled over, opinions. However, these opinions did not adequately meet my understanding of history, phenomenology and anthropology. It was Max Weber who was able to cut through my feelings and current experiences and explain to me in a rational and scientific manner how the holiness and power of God inevitably come to be expressed in the religion I see around me. Weber, nonetheless, only made sense after I returned to G. Van der Leeuw and Rudolf Otto to clarify the relationship of the characteristics of power and holiness to the idea of the numinous. First I will reflect on G. Van der Leeuw and let him clarify the role of power in religion. Then, moving to Otto for a fuller description of the numinous, I will reflect on his bonding of holiness to power in the idea of the numinous. Finally, I will let Weber explain the relationship of power and authority that brings holiness to the community under the gifts of the charismatic leaders.

Van der Leeuw and the Phenomenon of Power

Long before philosophers and theologians speculated about the nature of God as an "Other", individuals and tribes believed a power entered into their day-to-day life and indeed exerted special influence over them. In a letter written by R. H. Codrington[1] (later published in 1878 by Max Muller), we see this missionary describing the way the Melanesians addressed their idea of infinite power. They used the word mana. Codrington later defined mana as a power or influence not physical in itself but showing itself in physical force or power. The Melanesians and other South Sea Islanders strove to get this power to serve them as a personal benefit. Mana was considered variously as influence, strength, authority, intelligence, power and deity. These people did not distinguish the magical or supernatural from the powerful. If power was recognized in one's daily life, it was mana, and in the later evolution of religion, attributable to God.

In the development of South Seas religion and in various expressions of other religions we find that a "god" is accepted as both holy and powerful. Those that grow close to "god" and share in the mana of "god" possess holiness and power. Whenever anything great occurred that touched the people's lives, they attributed this benefit or wonder to mana. Not distinguishing secular acts from sacred acts[2] every extraordinary action generates the experience of power. Belief in this power originally was merely practical. Whether or not some sacred message or magical symbol hovered in the background was not of interest to the primitive peoples. The primitive person was comfortable with the idea that the whole universe had mana. When mana was manifested, according to a later understanding, it somehow pertained to God.

Power in itself was undifferentiated and possessed no moral value. The issue was to recognize power and to strive to interpret how power showed itself and interacted with or against other power (mana). The Sioux Indians believed in *wakanda*, in one instance an Originator, in another an impersonal power. Plants, animals and elements of nature had *wakanda* and would be described as both holy and powerful. From the Sioux to the Algonquins, to the Dyaks of Borneo, to the ancient Germans, and even to the Arabian notion of *Baraka*, power was always a strange gift, bordering on the supernatural. Sometimes the gift was confined to places, sometimes to people, or sometimes it lacked temporal or spatial characteristics. In any case, it was often seen as the basis of religion.[3]

Questions about the universe moved to questions about the power in the universe. As these questions deepened and became unified, they became the basic questions of religion. Nature, more than merely being concerned with life, was concerned with power. Why? Power was the background to life and a factor for any continuation of life. The Winnebago offered tobacco to any unusual object because it was *wakan* (a power). The idea of power was so basic to religion it is called a preanimistic concept. Because power is reflected upon only when it shows itself in some very striking manner, it arises in religion as a basic practical concern tied to the efficiency of day-to-day living. Eventually, this power strikes awe in people's minds and this power becomes linked to the sacred.

Primal Power

Power is not a personal element. It becomes universal energy. In a psychological sense it applies to humanity as superpersonal soul; in a cosmological sense, it assumes the form of divine agency immanently acting in the universe. Pantheism and monism become heirs to this experience. As religion evolves, power is seen as a manifestation of a unitary world order, appearing in conformity to rules or laws. Like Tao in China, Rta in India, Asha in Iran, Dike in Greece, various countries and cultures followed ordered systems that accounted for an all-inclusive measure of the universe and in themselves the systems possessed mana-like characteristics.

As the Greeks developed their religious sense, they sought primal unity and primal power as one, since they considered the essence of the universe to be power. From an immanent power dwelling in the universe, there developed a specific sense of divine power. The cosmological character of power gave rise to the psychological consideration related to the human soul and animism. In the Greco-Christian world the idea of power moved to the idea of single power by means of the concept of *pneuma* or spirit. The power of world-soul or *pneuma* overflowed into all things, among which is the human *pneuma* or spirit. Paul united the pneuma or life principle of humans with the psyche of divine power that touched men and women and gave them power or grace to be spiritual people. Once the Christian has this power of God, he can perform great miracles and wonders for the people. His deeds, thoughts, and values became represented as a store of power. In India this power is called *karma*, an impersonal treasure of power. Thus religion in the East and West joined psychology to cosmology, unifying human with cosmic power. This idea of power eventually developed into religious monism.

Philosophers see things as possessing their own potency and vitality. They have kinship with the primitive mind, recognizing things as bearers of power. An Ewe tribesman in West Africa enters the bush and finds a lump of iron. Returning home he falls ill. The priest visits him and explains that a *Tro*, a divine being, is manifesting its power in the iron. In the future, the iron should be worshipped. Thus, everything is potentially a bearer of power.

Power in early religious life sought description and identification. The religious person saw power everywhere in nature, but in order to be comfortable with this power he needed to explain how it fitted into the environment. Primitive man saw Dynamism as an attempt to understand the power of the environment and regarded Animism as an encounter between the will of the human person and the will of the power affecting him. From the experience of dreams, and the condition of bodies after death, the primitive sensed a soul as power that had an identification and thus a personality based on his will to interact. Logically, a form was sought for its expression. Meanwhile to the early religious person, the world was full of souls or spirits. Seas, lakes, mountains, trees, forests, villages, the heavens, and the underworld; all these possessed souls. Language described these elements as alive by saying, "The sea roars, the sun shines, and the heavens thunder." This personification by language showed the understanding of the primitive who wanted to relate these objects in such a way that he could find unity in the world. The religious person saw a will and a form in these powerful objects.[4] His efforts to connect all reality were basically religious, since it is the characteristic of religion to make sense out of all reality as much as it is humanly possible.

The problem of explaining the nature and expression of these souls is a distinct problem that we will not consider here. Cultures treated the souls of the dead and the spirits in things variously. Like a child looking at the world with a certain freshness and openness, the early religious person personified things and events in order to relate them readily to her personal life. We also seek to do the same. Because today we as individuals feel more and more solitary in our complex world, more alienated and adrift, we ask how can we interact with the powerful elements of the world. If we do not in some way identify them and relate their will and form to our lives, we suffer all the pain of isolation and emerging meaninglessness. Hence, today we too carry a type of Animism or Dynamism into our mysterious and fragile existence, hoping always that the events around us make sense.

While always desirous to find the earliest expressions of religion, let us content ourselves to accept animism and dynamism as two early significant forms of religious expression. The impersonal power of the *mana* moves to a sense of power that is supernatural and supreme in the universe. Moreover, as it touches human beings under the category of souls or spirits, it appears to have a will that stands as an object to be identified and related to human life and brings a form that shows need for the religious person to identify an interacting personality.[5]

Concretely, Jahweh is an animistic God, not because he originates from the mountain, or "personates" the wind, but because he is simply will, supreme activity, that over the years appears in the form of Jesus. The challenge of life is to respond first to power in itself, then to power with a will, and eventually to power with a form. The response is always our personal faith in the religion we see as satisfactory and as such clearly indicating this power in will and form.

A key problem today is the need to identify our religious attitudes among the powerful elements around us. Birth, marriage, and death indeed continue to have impact on our lives. But the seasons, and the land no longer touch us directly since agribusiness solves these problems related to the soil. For all practical purposes, food comes from a supermarket and is stored in our refrigerators. This hardly calls us to reflect on the powers of those elements that bring us food, such as the soil, the weather, the seeds, and the balance of seasons. Perhaps "the" power today is tied to nuclear power and economic power. On a practical level, the direct power in our lives is the power of the paycheck that later is transferred into personal checks and money that help us survive and flourish in our daily life. The economy of today has its own structures that set us apart from the economy of primitive life and the rural peasant experiencing his economy in agriculture or in hunting and food gathering. When we systematically reckon with the power subsisting in things, we call it fetishism.[6] Although mountains and trees are regarded as powerful and sacred, they do not qualify as such because a fetish is an object small enough that it can be carried around. One example is the Ark of the Covenant which stood for the power of God resting in the two tablets of stone. Pieces of wood etched with the outline of a totem serve also as fetishes. In these objects power subsists, but also overflows into the lives of humans related to the fetish. In view of this power we can understand the transition from the fetish to idols. Today, the concept of fetish is found in the mascot used as a power symbol for sports.

Tools and Weapons

To primitive people, work was always a creative enterprise. Tools consequently assumed an important role and carried with them a power wielded in use by the worker. In Africa and Indonesia, a smith is considered as one employing special powers in the use of his anvil and hammer. The gypsy, though misunderstood in our own time, will swear his oath on an anvil.

The weapon of battle is another implement that is powerful. In reality nothing more than a tool, such as an ax or hammer, the weapon received the veneration of warriors. The staff, for example, originally a weapon, later became the receptacle of royal power. The Roman church used it as a sign of episcopal power. When King Tutmosis III sent his general against Joppa, he gave him his sceptre which bore a special name and dignity. The Romans regarded the spear as a fetish of the god Mars. Whoever went to war invoked the sacred lance: *Mars vigila* ("Mars awake!"). The *hasta* and *ancile* (or shield) were believed to have come from heaven in the days of Numa. The Fox Indians also had a "sacred bundle" they considered to hold special protective powers. Both for individuals and tribes, objects considered precious were regarded as sacred and powerful, able to bring victory, peace, and

protection to the bearer. From Beowolf to Wagner, we celebrate
the special power of the hero's sword rendering its wielder invinci-
ble. When these objects were large, we saw them as idols, when
small, as amulets, when average sized and likened to tools, trea-
sures or weapons, the power shown was the power of a fetish.

Power of Taboo

Power shows itself in persons or things at any time or season.
Revealing itself often in wholly unexpected ways, power accepts
life and shows it to be a dangerous affair. When power does show
itself, the place, the person, the thing that reveals the power takes
on a special meaning. To describe this situation requires us to
come up with words like *mana*, *ieros*, and holy. The objects or persons themselves filled with power are called *tapu* (taboo?)[7] a word
from the same cultural domain as mana. *Tapu* means "exceptional."
The verb tapui means "to make holy." Implicit in the idea of tapu is
the idea of danger, caution, beware — all relating to the combined
ideas of holiness and power. In Greek life, the king and the
foreigner or stranger appeared as objects of *aidos*, or awe, with an
idea of *tabu*, as if receiving respect by keeping one's distance. In
Latin the word *hostis* means both a stranger and an enemy. One
may welcome or avoid the stranger, perhaps even kill the stranger
as an enemy. In any case, the outsider, the foreigner, the enemy is
not regarded with indifference. Hospitality, therefore, as well as
war, is a religious act intended either to repel or neutralize this
alien power.

Events that are surrounded by power such as war, hunting, and
sexual activity are described by elaborate tapu language, so that the
dignity of the power implicit in the event is respected. Violation of
tapu was not punished, because the power itself would react.
Power did not judge whether the offender was guilty or innocent.
The power acts something like electric current that simply shocks
anyone who touches the wire. [Note the story of Uzzah trying to
steady the Ark of the Covenant when it was being transported, (I
Cron. 13/9-11)]. Another example taken from Western culture is
the Romans who would cast traitors from the *Saxum Tarpeium*.

This was not a punishment, but a reaction of the Power. Whoever fell without dying would save his life. The *tribuni plebis*, as most holy leaders, were bearers of this type of execution which really was not to be considered an execution in the strict sense of the term.

The distance between the powerful and the powerless would show the relationship between the sacred and the profane (or secular). The sacred was powerful in its own right regardless of whether it seemed praiseworthy or good. The contrast was a reaction to the sacred with a sense of weakness or lack of value. The sacred, once recognized, brought a reaction of awe to those experiencing this power or force. Setting off the powerful from the powerless and the sacred from the profane is a basic reaction and response, as if constitutive of religious experience in all human activity.

Because *tabu* means a prohibition, power is shown as something to be respected if not avoided. Power is identified with the sacred. As such, the sacred releases feelings of fear, even hatred along with love and reverence. The *tabu* confronts a person experiencing this contradictory mixture of feelings, and commands the religious person to be cautious. The cautious activity is a reaction of awe that evolves into religious response. By paying attention to the awesome object or event, we engage in a positive observance of our awesome object. This observance is religious. By contrast, neglect would show a lack of a religious sense.

Otto and the Idea of the Holy

As Western believers, we move toward an appreciation of the sacred by focusing on our concept of God. Our Judeo-Christian origins call us to the concept of God as the specific one who is holy. By analogy to our experiences of human qualities, we think of this God as power, spirit, good, and complete unity, all contained under the idea of God as "The holy one." The word holy or sacred, however, need not be anchored in an idea of God alone. The Oriental person understands the sacred or holy under the heading of various religious ideas and values.

We approach the idea of holy in both a rational and nonrational way. We note, however, that the rational approach to the holy implies likewise a nonrational approach that becomes a more profound experience. Currently, we inquire into the durability of both approaches. In this inquiry, we find that religion in essence is estimated not merely under the rational experience.

Using the term numen as a symbol for holy (or holiness itself), we enter a discussion of special value that is at the heart of religion. When we as humans relate to holy as an idea and desire to approach the holy or the numinous, we shrink in humility. We see ourselves as opposite of holy, not merely in the moral sense of being sinful, but in the ontological sense of being profane or common. Our Judeo-Christian heritage takes the words of Isaiah, "I am a man of unclean lips" and Peter, "Depart from me for I am a sinful man, O Lord" and confirms our spirits in a self-depreciating response.

As sacred, the numinous has preeminently a transcendent character. To draw our attention, however, the numinous moves us to concepts that depict value. The terms that satisfy our need to value the numinous are august and fascinating. Value is not simply a moral term, it is a religious term in itself. In highly developed religions, the moral sense of duty and the religious sense of values stand side by side to the point of easily being confused. Consequently, the numinous in religion holds a transcendent characteristic with a value that is basically ontological.

Before the numinous, we feel humble and unworthy to approach. The danger in religion is to transfer this unworthiness or disvalue to the idea of moral weakness or sinfulness. Yet, basically, we respond to this sense of the numinous by desiring to be relieved of our weakness and unworthiness. We want to be delivered from our profane position into the holiness of the numinous. This deliverance or redemption is not a moral issue in itself. It is theological, especially for the Jew and Christian who see God as the all holy one whom they wish to approach. They stand in awe before the *tremendum*, hesitating to approach until the numinous prepares them by covering up their profaneness (i.e., in the sense of atonement) and making them holy so that they can be in the company of the holy.

Rudolf Otto (*The Idea of the Holy*) penetrates the term holy and calls this term the "overplus" of meaning. As such, it confronts the religious mind as holy (agios, sanctus, or qadosh) in the tradition that can clarify or merge with the word numen. Otto discourages us from further investigation of the holy unless we have had a religious experience. In response, many of us wonder if we dare proceed further, but then most of us feel that we have been especially close to the numinous at various times in our lives. One example might be a worship service. What is so unique about a sacred experience during worship? Common to other experiences such as the experience of gratitude, worship has a potential to move beyond the ordinary and the common to the unique experience we call religious. Schleiermacher calls the religious experience of a Westerner the feeling of absolute dependence. This sense of dependence is difficult to describe, but as we think of Abraham (Gen. 18/27), we appreciate how he speaks of his dependence on God as total and complete. To Otto, a proper religious experience that inculcates a feeling of lasting dependence is the genuine sense of the numen or numinous.

For Christians and Jews, the holy or the numen is rationally stabilized in the image of God. As Westerners, we need not worry about this mental process, but we still need to face the issue of describing the word numen in greater detail. Otto[8] lists three general concepts providing support for the description of numen:

1) Tremendum - deserving to be feared

2) Mysterium - mystery

3) Fascinosum - attractive or fascinating

All of these three ideas are interrelated as they contribute to the deepening understanding of the term numen or sacred.

Tremendum

Reflecting on the power of the word *tremendum*, we sift the synonyms most helpful to our understanding. Awe is a practical and timely word that links us to our Jewish heritage. The Jews spoke of holy dread (hiqdish), but the traditional word of Jewish Wisdom literature is fear. "The beginning of knowledge (wisdom) is fear of the Lord" (Prov. 1/7). The holiness of God is respected, appreciated and somewhat understood in the idea of fear. Not as the state of being afraid, but as a holy dread, a hallowed sense of respectful fear (e.g., Job 9/34). The Latin uses the term augustus or august for the same sense of respect.

G. Van der Leeuw recounts how the Romans linked the word numen to the idea of power. When we think of the exercise of power in our daily life, we notice our organizational tendencies to go to the source of power. When we have a question, or need to find a solution for a problem, we ask: "Who is the head of this organization? Who is in charge? Who has the decision-making power here?" Almost instinctively, we look towards the "boss" or head of the outfit for a solution. This attitude goes back to the Romans, who called the source of power, the head, or *caput*, the legal person, the one who had the authority to act and decide. The Romans saw the exercise of power as the *nod* of the head, which they referred to with the word *numen*.[9] Eventually, the Romans gave this legal person of power a personality and attributed this power to the array of gods who were part of the daily life of the Romans.

Estimating the character of awe and respect for the numen, we find that the sense of awe can be quiet or loud, soft or demonstrative. Linked to this awe is *orge Theou* (ὀργή Θεοῦ) or the wrath of God. Again, this wrath of God is not a moral concern, but enhances the idea of God's holiness. Most of these terms do not make sense except to a person who has had some sort of a religious experience and possesses the openness of a child that can readily accept God as powerful, striking immense awe in our hearts, holy, wrathful, but not directly appealing to our own sense of sinfulness. This term wrath (orge) is supernatural or nonrational to our experience. Another term we can supply here is majesty or overpowering strength. The idea of numinous exists in the word majesty itself.

In many religions, the numinous with its awesome power is particularly exemplified in mountains. Remote and unapproachable, often volcanic and repellant, in all cases majestic, the mountains stand apart from the ordinary, incorporating the power of the Wholly Other along with the idea of holiness. Greece has its Olympus, France its Mt. Blanc, the U. S. has Mt. McKinley and Mt. Rainier. Every region has its holy peak. The oldest heaven in religion has been the mountain top. In the Old Testament deity dwells on the mountain (Ps. 89/12) whether it be Tabor, Hermon, or Sinai. The mountain, its hard stone and dramatic shape, brought to it our special regard as the primal and permanent element of the world. Thus the habits of religious expression built up over the centuries show the numinous as both holy and powerful, awesome and majestic, mysterious and extraordinary.

The Numinous In Animals

Chesterton said that we erroneously talk of wild animals. The human person is the only wild animal. It is only human life that breaks out and "disobeys" nature and acts contrary to his nature.[10] All other animals are tame animals, following with respectability the rules of their tribe. The animal is both foreign and familiar to the human person. As such, humans regard animals as possessing both sacred and profane powers. The animal on the one hand brings awe and on the other intimacy to the daily life of each of us. The result is a mixture of animal cults and Totemism. The animal consequently is seen equally as numinous, mysterious and comprehensible to our daily experience. The strangest animal is perhaps the snake, the most familiar is the domesticated beast (e.g., pig, cow or dog). For the Hindu, the cow is sacred, never to be killed by human hands.

The distinction between human and animal blurs with various tribes and cultures. In fairy tales and in Totemistic culture of both North and South American Indians, the animal and human person are bound by treaty, war and key events touching human life. Remembering the "Wolfman" films of the '30s and the recent film called "Ladyhawk" (1985), we find in several cultures the comfortable transposition between human and animal forms. In brief, the animal is seen as the "other" to which the human flees for refuge and comfort. In the dance, the animal mask provided strength for the human dancer reaching for the numinous in his life. It helped him identify with the power emanating from the animal. Walt Whitman says in "Song of Myself":

> I think I could turn and live with animals, they are so placid and self-contain'd,
> I stand and look at them long and long.
>
> They do not sweat and whine about their condition,
> They do not lie awake in the dark and weep for their sins,
> They do not make me sick discussing their duty to God,
> Not one is dissatisfied, not one is demented with the mania of owning things,
> Not one kneels to another, nor to his kind that lived thousands of years ago,
> Not one is respectable or unhappy over the whole earth.
>
> So they show their relations to me and I accept them,
> They bring me tokens of myself, they evince them plainly in their possessions.

Here is a religious sense that sharply separates the human from the animal, but raises in the human a respect for the condition of the animal as possessing features that should not be cut off totally from human life.

As we look at the examples of numinous in the world around us from celestial life to mountains, animals and persons, we realize that worship in the experiences of the community always depends on the substantiation of power and awe arising from the belief of the individuals.

Mysterium

Mysterium supports the word *tremendum*. Schleiermacher uses the idea of dependence as a sense of or an awareness of the mystery of God and of our created condition in relation to this mystery.

The mystic in a nonthreatening way builds a self-depreciation to identify his place in the world with a Creator God described as *tremendum* or as the fullness of being. The mystic moves on slowly but boldly to identify himself with the transcendent, all powerful reality. Such a sense of dependence incorporates a sense of optimism in being a creature and a part of this fullness of life, the *mysterium tremendum*.

An analysis of the term *mysterium*, or mystery, reminds us of Otto's reference to Tersteegen's statement: "A comprehended God is no God."[11] In a natural sense, mystery is a secret uncomprehended and unexplained. In a religious sense, mystery is a wholly other (alienum) as foreign and incomprehensible. In our normal experiences, a foreigner in our midst will stand out and will call attention to our defensive attitudes. As the mystery is absorbed, there arises a stupor or a special sense of respect for the nonrational elements of the mystery. This stupor in turn leads to an aspiration for the void or nothingness that the transcendent mystery possesses.

Fascinosum
The numinous first calls up ideas of awe and majesty (*mysterium tremendum*), but eventually and in harmony with these ideas it calls attention to its attractive or fascinating character. There is a strange affinity between awe and fascination. If we call fascination a nonrational term of experience of the numinous, on the rational side we can use words like: love, mercy, pity and comfort. In our daily rational experience, we can appreciate how a lover evokes both a sense of awe (fear, dread) and attraction (fascination). The tremendum comes first and later fascination follows.

One further term used for fascination is dire or weird (deinos or dirus). If with Sophocles we accept that "much there is that is weird, but nought is weirder than man,"[12] so also must we accept that the experience of the numen deserves to be called weird.

In religious practice, the believer desires to possess the numen and is in danger of employing thinly veiled artificial means of asceticism. As each religious person wants to experience the mysterium, the religious "life" can be sought as an end in itself. Basically, asceticism is not meant to be an end but rather a means to an end. Easily, the "religious" person might become mesmerized by the mystery and the fascination of the numinous and fail to understand her or his identity in relationship to this numinous object.

Otto describes how the rational and nonrational elements in this sense of *mysterium tremendum* and *fascinosum* mix. The rational can be described as an experience of grace, conversion, or second birth. The nonrational elements can be described simply as a sense of closeness to God. Obviously, the nonrational is difficult to describe in any detail, but then how do you explain to a materialist the value of the sensation of joy at the hearing of a symphony? Deep down in our hearts do we not admit that the nonrational sense of the numinous is more important to us?

The mystery of the numinous sets up a basic relationship between that which evokes awe and fascination (or fear and attraction). No amount of words will explain how the two concepts are inherently related, but the investigation of each element should give greater insight into the meaning of the related terms. On the level of aesthetics, we see a remarkable painting that, like the numinous, is sublime. As such, it is both daunting and attracting. Its appreciation both humbles and exalts us. Both qualities are related, conjoined, but not connected. The challenge remains: how do we identify the association of *tremendum* and *fascinosum*, and how do we recognize both rational and nonrational characteristics in the numen? The answer to this question comes partially from the understanding of the principle that ideas "attract" one another, and one idea can call another into consciousness. (The same principle applies to feelings.) Add to this the experience of influences from custom or from moral obligation arising in the super-ego (or the parent image) in the human personality, a curious mixture of ideas can arise and interact in the mind. Opposites are likely candidates for this experience. The association of one idea to another can set up lasting combinations and associations of one to another that develop a certain permanent pattern, in turn influencing and causing new ideas to emerge. Based on the principle of association, we can reasonably appreciate how the rational and nonrational elements and feelings relate to each other in the sense of the sacred as *tremendum* and *fascinosum*.

The experience of music is a clear example of how ideas interact and how rational and nonrational elements interact. Each approaches the sublime or numinous in music from his or her own experiences and previous association of ideas. Each person estimates the impact of music from his rational being and from his nonrational sensitivities. Music provides definite, if elusive, analogies corresponding with our nonmusical life. The musical consciousness can clarify and certify values in our nonmusical everyday consciousness. Eventually, we acknowledge a fabric of life seen partially in the threads of music as the woof and in the human feelings as the warp. The music in its entirety is the rationalized schema of reality. The human feelings responding to the music constitute the nonrational side of the musical experience. Musical feelings like numinous feelings are something wholly other and cannot be clearly analyzed or given to clear rational explanation.

Eventually, we sense the holy as a dignity we can share or even possess, but we shrink from the arrogance that we are holy or like unto God in spite of the encouragement coming from the creation accounts of Genesis. Meanwhile, we ask how the power of religion moves into our world and overtakes our personal life. Drawing back, we acknowledge that the issue of power in religion cannot hide from the scrutiny of society. Our surest ally in this struggle is active society and its exercise of checks and balances in everyday life.

Weber and the Legitimation of Power

Power As Legitimate In Religion

Religious activity, because it is an activity that involves a social relationship, must be guided by the belief in the existence of a legitimate order.[13] This order is the basis for power in the external expression of religion. The order will be valid only if it is oriented towards determinable "maxims" or norms. Once an order develops the prestige of being considered binding, it attains the stable position of legitimacy. Tradition, need, and expediency are various motives that society finds for making an order "binding" or highly legitimate. Weber shows this idea of legitimacy under the schema of the bases of legitimacy. He states that persons may ascribe legitimacy in a social order by virtue of four categories:

1) Tradition: Validity pertains to that which has always been. This is the oldest and most universal type of legitimacy.

2) Affectual Faith: Validity pertains to that newly revealed or exemplary reality.

3) Value-rational faith: Validity pertains to that deduced as absolute. The purest type of this example is natural law.

4) Positive enactment: Believed to be legal, it is derived from:
   A) Voluntary agreement of interested parties, or
   B) Imposed by an authority held to be legitimate.

Tradition as the oldest and most universal type of legitimacy was always sacred. To depart from tradition meant a new sacred power took over and established a new order. This new order arose from prophetic oracles or pronouncements sanctioned by prophets. Conformity depended on belief in the legitimacy of the prophet, who now expressed a new position of power and sacrality. Today, the most common form of legitimacy is the belief in legality.

Power and Domination

Power in a social relationship means that one person is in a position to carry out his own will despite resistance. This implies that power here is individualized in a person or small group of persons in the social relationship. Domination, by contrast, is the probability that a command will be obeyed by a given group of persons. Power is sociologically amorphous, but domination is more precise and gives the probability that a command will be obeyed. If an organization possesses an administrative staff, to some degree this organization is based on domination.[14]

Every genuine form of domination implies a minimum of voluntary compliance. That is, one is willing to obey because of ulterior motives. Normally, the type of motives determines the type of domination. Also, a further critical element that allows domination is a belief in legitimacy.[15] In order to dominate, a social system must cultivate a belief in its legitimacy. From the kind of legitimacy that is claimed, arises the type of obedience given to the social system.

Three Types of Domination as Authoritative

Weber lists three types of legitimate domination as authoritative whose claims to legitimacy are based on:

1) Traditional Grounds: resting on the belief in the sanctity of immemorial tradition (Traditional Authority).

2) Charismatic Grounds: resting on the devotion to the exceptional sanctity, heroism, or exemplary character of an individual person, and of the norms or order revealed by him (Charismatic Authority).

3) Rational Grounds: resting on belief in the legality of the rules (Legal-Rational Authority).

Weber shows the role of holiness in the first two of the three categories. By contrast, legal authority holds a rational basis of an organization that is more abstract, impersonal, and aloof, exercising its domination through a bureaucratic administrative staff. One of the problems in organizations is size. Once an organization becomes large and complex, it needs bureaucratic administration to accomplish its basic goals. The quest for efficiency today designates monocratic bureaucracy as the most capable system of attaining efficiency and the most rational means of exercising authority over human persons. Yet, we should not overlook the nonrational power in traditional and charismatic authority. We are drawn to religion and its authoritative domination frequently on the supra-rational or nonrational level no matter how large the structure may be.

Traditional Authority

Believed by virtue of the sanctity of age-old rules and powers, traditional authority is primarily based on personal loyalty which results from common upbringing. Members and staff equally obey the master out of loyalty to the tradition in itself and the master's ability to carry out this tradition in areas free of specific rules. When rule is organized in the hands of elders, there is a distinct respect for rulers who are most familiar with the sacred traditions. This type of gerontocratic rule respects sharply the means of getting in touch with the sacred. When the organization is small, its traditional authority is patriarchal. As it grows, it becomes patrimonial, and eventually it becomes feudal, moving forward to gradual decentralization and complex government.

Charismatic Authority

Weber applies the term charism to persons considered extraordinary and endowed with "supernatural, superhuman, or at least specifically exceptional powers or qualities."[16] This sociological description is not far from the theological treatment of charism which further describes the term as a gift meant for the service to the community. Paul (I Cor. 12-14) places charisms in the ordered life of the community and understands them as characteristic of baptized Christians in general. Strangely enough, Karl Rahner designates the hierarchy in the institutional church as endowed with the role of giving the final assessment and verdict on the exercise of charisms in the community. Yet at times this same hierarchy must be corrected by the charismatic element in the church.[17] This dramatic tension between institutional domination and charism shows a further delineation of power as each exercises her or his charism in the community.

Weber notes that in primitive circumstances this peculiar quality was considered to be rooted in the magical powers or wisdom of the various leaders or heroes in the community. For Weber it is not the authority structure that is important to a charism, but what was singularly important was the way the charismatic individual was regarded by those subject to his or her charismatic authority as a follower, disciple, or fellow believer. Only if there is belief in the rightness of the charism is the charism operative and legitimate. There must be a response of belief on the part of the people. If the charismatic leader seems to lose his magical power, and if his leadership fails to benefit his followers, Weber states that it is likely his charismatic authority will disappear. This is the appropriate understanding of the divine right of kings. Hence the Pauline and Christian idea of charism is close to that of Weber's in relation to the charism's need to be of benefit to the community.

Charismatic Community

When an organized group chooses to subject itself to charismatic authority, it is called a charismatic community. Weber considers this group to be based on an emotional form of community relationship. The administrative staff does not consist of "officials." The staff is chosen in terms of the charismatic qualities of its members. Consequently, characteristics of appointment, salary, promotion, and dismissal are absent. With no hierarchical structure, the leader merely intervenes when he considers the members of his staff lacking in charismatic qualifications for a given task. In Christian history, the charismatic community evolved towards a hierarchy in the second and fourth centuries, and to the hieracracy in the twelfth century and forward.

The followers in a charismatic community live primarily in a communal relationship with their leader and are supported by means of voluntary gifts. The leader preaches, and lays down obligations by virtue of his revelation, inspirations, or own will. In case of conflict with a competing authority, some kind of contest must be held to resolve the conflict. In effect, only one leader can be right in such a conflict; the other must be guilty or wrong.

Because charismatic authority repudiates the past, it tends to be a revolutionary force. It recognizes no traditional positions of power. Moreover, it repudiates traditional involvement in the daily structure of the world. Its basis of legitimacy is its own personal charism so long as it is proved and recognized to be charismatic.[18] The famous leaders of mendicant orders, such as Francis and Dominic, belong to this category. No doubt many others qualify as charismatic down through the centuries. We see the qualities of a charismatic as we reflect on Arthur O'Shaughnessy's poem, "Ode":

> We are the music-makers,
>   And we are the dreamers of dreams,
> Wandering by lone sea-breakers,
>   And sitting by desolate streams;
> World-losers and world-forsakers,
>   On whom the pale moon gleams:
> Yet we are the movers and shakers
>   Of the world forever. It seems.
>
> With wonderful deathless ditties
>   We build up the world's great cities,
> And out of a fabulous story
>   We fashion an empire's glory:
> One man with a dream, at pleasure,
>   Shall go forth and conquer a crown:
> And three with a new song's measure
>   Can trample an empire down.
>
> We, in the ages lying
>   In the buried past of the earth,
> Built Nineveh with our sighing,
>   And Babel itself with our mirth:
> And o'erthrew them with prophesying
>   To the old of the new world's worth
> For each age is a dream that is dying,
>   Or one that is coming to birth.

The Institutionalization of Charismatic Leadership

When the tide that lifted a charismatically led group out of everyday life flows back into the channels of worldly routines, at least the "pure form" of charismatic life will wane and turn into an institution. Inevitably, the charismatic following of a war leader will be transformed into a state, and the charismatic community of a prophet, artist, or philosopher will become a church, sect, academy, or school. When charism is exposed to the condition of everyday life, it is like exposing vintage wine to the open air. A change occurs. The fresh charismatic message ultimately becomes dogma, doctrine, rule, law, or petrified tradition.

In the process of institutionalization, the basically antagonistic forces of charisma and tradition merge. Beyond mere rational regulation, both charisma and tradition rest on a sense of loyalty and dedication to the leader. Because both believe in the sanctity of the individual leader, both show a religious affinity that draws them to a logical harmonization. Here again we see the connection between power and holiness.

The social relationships directly involved in a charismatic community are indeed so personal that charismatic authority is completely foreign to ordinary everyday routine structures. In its pure form, charismatic authority is transitory and evolving. It cannot remain stable. When it does move towards institutionalization or routinization, it will be considered — according to Weber — either traditionalized or rationalized. This routinization allows for a clearer understanding of the religious tension in charismatic expression between: the extraordinary or other-worldly and the ordinary or this-worldly (mundane). The routinization among other things attempts to make grace, considered as a sacred gift of God, available to everyone on a routine basis in everyday life.

Choice of a Successor

The idea of change in a charismatic community becomes critical when the problem of replacing the charismatic leader arises. The problem can be met in various ways:

1) Search for a new charismatic leader on the basis of certain criteria.

2) Select a leader by lot, by oracle, or by divine revelation.

3) Let the original leader choose his successor.

4) Let a charismatically qualified staff choose a leader.

5) Let the charism be transmitted by heredity.

   In this case recognition of charismatic qualities in the individual is no longer required, but the position becomes charismatic and is legitimated by hereditary succession. Hereditary monarchy is a conspicuous illustration.

6) Let the charism be transmitted by ritual.

   One example is the transmission of priestly charism by the laying on of hands. As in hereditary transmissions above, the idea of charism is dissociated from that of a particular individual.

In these latter two cases legitimacy is no longer directed to the individual but to the acquired qualities by means of heredity or ritual acts.

Along with the problem of succession to the original charismatic leader is the desire on the part of the administrative staff in carrying on the charism. In time, only a small group of loyal followers or staff members will be prepared to devote their lives purely and idealistically to their call. The great majority will need a more traditionalized community in order to meet their material needs of everyday living. Eventually, norms will be set for the recruitment and training of followers in the original charismatic community. Later on, offices and benefices will be established and the anti-economic character of the community will be altered and brought under some fiscal management.

A free election of a successor to a charismatic leader serves sharply to eliminate that which is esteemed. Hence, the followers may need to wait for a qualified successor who can in some fashion replace the charismatic leader. Roman magistrates designated their successors from many qualified persons before the assembled army proclaimed them leaders. The designation of a dictator in the field during military emergencies that called for an extraordinary person remained for a long time in Rome a characteristic remnant of the old pure type of charismatic selection.

If the charismatic leader has not designated a successor, it may easily occur to the ruled, the disciples, and followers that they themselves are best suited to recognize a qualified successor. Since the disciples at this point have complete control over the instruments of power, they do not find it difficult to appropriate this role as a right. We note again that since the effectiveness of charisma rests on the faith of the ruled, their approval of a designated successor is indispensible.

In the patrimonial or feudal state, designation of a successor by the closest and most powerful vassals and acclamation by the ruled is normally the result of this mode of choosing a successor. The so-called election of a new king, pope, or bishop through designation by disciples and close followers and the subsequent popular acclamation was indeed not an election in our modern sense of the term, but a practical selection process giving recognition to a qualification older than the election process, that of a charism recognized by the designators and acclaimers alike.

Weber believed that whenever the charismatic community entered the path of electing their rulers, the electoral process would ultimately be tied to norms. In this way, the genuine roots of charisma having disappeared, they would now be replaced by a tradition of norms that provide for the sanctity of the process lost by the ending of the charismatic rule. As the norms develop, the designation process becomes more detailed, and tied to structures and acclamation by the ruled, it moves into the background (e.g., election of a pope). This discussion of the evolution of the selection points up the fate of charisma, as it begins to recede into history with the development of permanent institutional structures. What happens in the process is the depersonalization of charisma. As this process moves forward, the charisma is transformed into a new quality that is either: transferable, personally acquirable, or attached to the incumbent of an office or to an institutional structure. The most common case of a depersonalization of charisma is the belief in transferability through blood ties. The idea of individual inheritance only comes later in culture. Primarily, the immortality of the household needed to be considered. Charisma was handed down to keep the household intact and, furthermore, certain households rose above others when charismatic endowments seemed to be recognized. From this basic idea of household structure we move to royal and aristocratic powers.

Charisma was acquired in a variety of ways depending on one's position as a magician, rain-maker, or medicine man, or as one having political authority. With the development of cult there arose charismatic blood ties between certain priestly positions. By developing systems that continued in time, the charismatic spirit was able to be considered a force in the ongoing communities.

Once the belief arose that charism is bound to blood relationship, its meaning is altogether reversed. If originally a man was ennobled by virtue of his own actions, now only the deeds of his forefathers could legitimate him.[19] As charism more and more becomes part of an institution and is transferred by blood, ceremony, magic, or ordination, the distinctive heroic gifts of the individual endowed with charism fade into the past.

In the early Christian church, the Bishop of Rome occupied an essentially charismatic position. The church of Rome quite early acquired a specific authority that asserted itself time and again against the intellectual superiority of the Hellenistic Orient. The Eastern church producing most of the great church fathers, established doctrines and held all the ecumenical councils. They allowed the impression to grow in the West that God would not permit the church of the world capitol to err despite its much smaller intellectual accomplishments.

In time as the church of the West became more bureaucratized, it considered the Bishop of Rome to enjoy charisma by reason of office, not merely as an incumbent. Centuries later, the Puritans rejected office charisma, but the Catholic church continued to accept it as it carried on the distinction between the charism of office and the worthiness of the person in the office. In this distinction, a highly structured church could risk having a depraved priest or bishop as long as the power and charism of office remained intact and gave support to the institution.

As a rule, the routinization of a charismatic community will bring some conflict. The power of the leader will now be seen in a new light by force of selection, succession, or ritual. Doubts will arise about the force of charism shown in the newly developed community. The office of the leader will take on new powers as the need for security is gradually met. The best example of designation of a successor by charismatic followers of the leader is found in the election of bishops and particularly the bishop of Rome. The election of kings in Europe is a parallel example. One of the chief forces behind the stabilization of a charismatic community is the need for economic stability. Along with the ideal of loyalty to the charismatic leader, allegiance to hereditary leaders in particular is strongly influenced by the consideration that all inherited and legitimately acquired property would be endangered if people stopped believing in the sanctity of hereditary succession to the throne. Here practicality, the need for stability and economic considerations merge to create a valid basis for the holiness of office to be respected. Once routinization or stabilization occurs, holiness as a power and power as a sign of holiness is transferred from the charismatic leader to the office which is shown in the position of the successor.

Weber's Idea of Domination

To understand *in globo* the impact of power on religion, we should review Weber's outline concerning domination as shown in his work, *Economy and Society.*

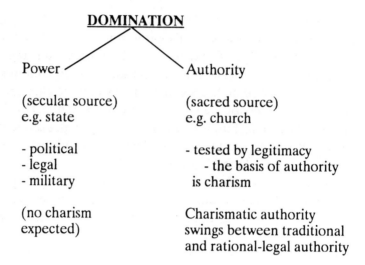

DOMINATION

Power   Authority

(secular source)   (sacred source)
e.g. state   e.g. church

- political   - tested by legitimacy
- legal   - the basis of authority
- military   is charism

(no charism   Charismatic authority
expected)   swings between traditional
                              and rational-legal authority

In all of society, in both historical and evolutionary perspective, there exists this internal double competition between power and authority as best exemplified in the West in the modern state and the church. The state has power in the physical control of resources. No charism is inherent in power simply because some group has this power (macht) that is best exemplified in political and legal power.

By contrast, authority in religion (e.g. the church) must be legitimated. Because a community believes in the rightness of the authority, it is legitimate. The basis for this legitimacy in general is charism, which in turn sets up an ongoing tension between:

person	-	office
sect	-	church
prophet	-	priest
monastic orders	-	hierarchy

When the charism found at first in an individual is stabilized or routinized, there is a tendency to snuff out its spirit. What actually happens is that the charism with all its nonstructured tendencies flares up again like a dramatic forest fire temporarily smoldering underground until it finds some way to reach the surface. Again, we must reconsider that a charism is incomplete until the community responds and legitimates it. Then the charism has its authority to act, truly a power of no small magnitude and usually it is originally found in the individual person.

Holiness fits into this discussion as we reflect that the spirit of holiness identified in the West with the Ultimate, or Supreme Being, is shared in the human community. Those that live out the holiness of God are often called upon to show this holiness by expressing their possession of a gift or a variety of gifts under the heading of charism or charisma. When a religious group sees these gifts at work in their midst and wishes to accept them, then they legitimate these gifts and the authority (power) of the charism is at work in the midst of the community through these gifts. As these gifts show themselves, we have the context for understanding how religious experiences are found in a community and in individuals. The numinous, or spirit of God, is alive in the midst of the community. As such, we have holiness concretely showing itself, but charism calls attention to the way the community can see this holiness. As the charism functions, the power (and authority) of God is functioning in the power of the charismatic expression.

The authentic power, therefore, of religion will come through the charisms, first found usually in the individual, (e.g. prophet) before the charism is routinized, and later taken up by the community in the structures. Obviously, the abuse of power in religion is found when the leaders of the routinized charism's community misuse this charism now transferred to an office or role such as enjoyed by the bishop, priest, or preacher in Christianity.

Further Comments on Charism

Ordinary needs of everyday economic and political routines are satisfied by the bureaucracy and its earlier example of rational order, the patriarchical structure. All extraordinary needs, i.e. those that transcend the everyday economic routines, are satisfied by charismatic authority. Going back into history, we find that the natural leaders who emerge in times of distress — whether political, religious or economic — were neither appointed office holders nor professionals, but were bearers of special gifts called charisms.

In contract to bureaucratic organization, charisma knows no formal and regulated appointment or dismissal, no career advancement, or salary, no local or technical jurisdiction. Charisma is self-determined and sets its own limits. The charismatic leader seizes the task and demands that others follow and obey him by virtue of this mission. If those to whom he feels missioned (sent) do not respond, his claim to charism collapses. While the charismatic does not derive his claims to charism from the will of his followers, as if by election, yet once his charismatic activity is established, it becomes the duty of the people to recognize[20] his charisma.

In its expression, charisma is a highly individual quality. Opposite of bureaucracy, in respect to economic substructure, charisma does not depend on continuous income, and at times abhors the owning of property or possessions, e.g. Francis of Assisi. The charismatic lives in the world, not off the world. Sometimes the charismatic leader may seek out booty or plunder, but Weber reminds us that in the profile of a charismatic, we will see a rejection of all methodical rational acquisition of property. While the patriarchical structure looks to an orderly household, the charismatic receives the required means of support through sponsors or voluntary contributions and gifts. By its nature, charisma is not a continuous institution, and its authority is inherently unstable and fleeting. In pure charisma, the mission of the leader may be short-lived; his legitimacy lasts only as long as his personal strength is active and proven. When the people withdraw their support, the leader becomes a private citizen.

Evolution and Charism

Bureaucratic structures often set in motion major revolutionary forces, but the bureaucracy revolutionizes with technical means, and from "without." First it changes the material or social order, and as a consequence, the people are changed. Charisma, by contrast, rests upon the belief in revelation and in heroes, and upon the conviction that certain manifestations--be they religious, artistic, scientific, or political--are important in themselves. Resting on this conviction in the leader, charisma will revolutionize persons from "within," and shape material and social conditions according to this revolutionary will.

The revolutionary power of charism shows itself much more dramatically than the power of the bureaucratic structures. While the bureaucratic structure believes that it can change rules, norms, and traditions, even those held as sacred for a long period of time, charisma in its most potent form disrupts rational rule and overturns all ideas of sanctity. Instead of reverence for customs that are ancient, and therefore sacred, charism enacts a new inner subjection to the unprecedented and unique. In effect, charisma speaks directly for the divine. In a purely empirical and value-free sense, charisma is the distinctly creative revolutionary force of history.[21]

Charismatic power rests on personal devotion to the leader. This holds true for patriarchical power, but stands in sharp contrast to the power of appointed leaders of the bureaucratic order. Also, in comparison with the patriarch enjoying authority as a bearer of norms, the charismatic leader enjoys loyalty and authority by virtue of his mission embodied in him. The mission may not necessarily be revolutionary, but in most cases charisma inverts hierarchies and overthrows custom, law and tradition.

Communal Life

Next to the household, charisma is the second important representative of communal living characterized here as the absence of goals of production and consumption. Fully developed, this communal living becomes either "spoils community" of the camp, or a "monastery community" of love.

Since charisma is extraordinary, and noneconomic in its power, its vitality becomes endangered when everyday economic interests become predominant, as we find threatening our world today. The power of charism is fragile since it can never withhold its unqualified permission to found families or to engage in economic pursuits. It thrives on a love of danger as we find in military life, and a

love of unworldly discipleship as we find in the church that will preserve charisms for the future.

The rarity and short-lived experience of charisma force us to
soberly regard this phenomenon as ineluctably set on a course from
a turbulently exciting life that knows no economic rationality to a
slow death by suffocation under the weight of material interests. In
terms of our present complex engaging economic systems, the
question is: Can charisma possibly exist, or much more, be able to
thrive, or rather is it doomed to end soon in our world culture as
we know it today?

Because charisma has been found in church leaders in the West
since the time of Christ, we can readily see the danger of charisma
becoming suffocated by the highly organized bureaucratic structures of the clergy-led church. As long as we have bureaucratic authority, the issues of extending ordination to women and married
persons will survive only as a suitable topic for institutional church
discussion under this complex bureaucracy. Once we see charisma
as deeper and more distinct than the question of changing the
structural requirements for ordination, we will open our eyes to the
possibilities of charismatic persons standing out in the community
in a variety of effective ways well accepted as expressing a mission
of importance for all who profess allegiance to Western
Christianity.

Summary

The mystery of religion leads us into many questions, but one
impelling question that recurs again and again in the literature is:
How do holiness and power relate to each other as expressions of
this very human experience called religion? Initially, I experienced
both holiness and power in religion as compatible characteristics,
but both appeared to become separated as my life in Christianity
moved forward in time. Eventually, I asked why are they become
separated? Why do the powerless seem to be so holy, and why are
the powerful religious leaders so lacking in holiness? G. Van der
Leeuw, Rudolf Otto, and Max Weber provided the understanding

of holiness and power as compatible and correlative terms germain to the study of religion.

G. Van der Leeuw comments on the central position of the term power in all religions. Variously described as *mana, wakanda,* or *Baraka,* this power is a strange phenomenon always bordering on the supernatural, always used to describe the activity of the universe and its integral elements. As religion evolved, power is seen as a sign of unitary world order that is connected harmoniously to the other elements of its belief system whether monistic or pantheistic. The human person in his creative activity of work or his defensive activity of war cooperated with this power in order to survive and flourish. As exceptional, these elements of power were related to the holiness of God. The elaborate tapu language surrounding the special activities of hunting, of war, and of sexual relationships called for respect and awareness of the roots of this power in the all-powerful and holy God.

Otto in his *The Idea of the Holy* talks about the common understanding of numinous as a mystery, that is both tremendous and fascinating. Each of these three ideas describes the experience of the holy in the average person's life. Respecting both rational and nonrational elements, each person senses in the idea of the holy a harmonization of a variety of concepts that relate how this numinous Ultimate Reality touches our own personal lives and comes to be understood as a factor in our daily experience.

The Ultimate dominates our lives and calls us to feel completely dependent in our relationship of awe and fear, august mystery and overpowering majesty. This idea of God as numinous and sacred calls up all sorts of descriptive words showing us that we are quite inarticulate as we search for a means of expression.

From the sense of power in G. Van der Leeuw and of holiness in Otto, we move to a sense of the unity of power and holiness as Weber unfolds the idea of legitimacy. Once religion shows itself in society, it attempts to express the holy as a source of power that moves into the everyday life of the believer. The legitimacy of power comes primarily from the dominating authority of charisma. From an individual person with extraordinary or superhuman powers, gifts so unique that a group of disciples willingly follow, obey, believe, and by their belief legitimate this power, we view the clearest beginnings of power in a communal religious setting. The charismatic leader evolves towards more and more organization. In time, sacred traditions are established, and these in turn are supported by a legal-rational organization that follows.

The initial power of the charismatic leader filters down through the community. The power becomes depersonalized and often blurred by the complexities of the organization. But always with a sense of history, the community can look back to the holiness of the charismatic leader as a mediator of the holiness of the numinous and a source of sacred traditions to follow. When the charismatic leader dies, a new situation arises: namely that of choosing a replacement to carry on the sacred work of the community begun by the leader. Once routinization of the community occurs, holiness as a power and power as a sign of holiness is transferred from the charismatic leader to the office that is established by the position of the successor.

Just as power and authority compete with one another in Weber's historical description of Western social activity, so do the state and church compete for domination over society as a whole. In religion, charismatic authority legitimates the power of the numinous coming down to the people through a gifted or charismatic leader. Belief in this charisma is always critical for the continuation of this authoritative power. Generally, charisma is short-lived. Religious society with a practical will to survive allows this charism to swing between the traditions that are carried forward and the rational-legal authority that brings gifts into the complex society wanting to stabilize the sense of the numinous in the office now routinized by the charismatic community.

The sense of the numinous is an awesome experience. Most of us cannot follow closely for any length of time the life of the charismatic leader who seems so close to the numinous. The everyday tasks of maintaining economic and political stability draw us away from the ethereal atmosphere of the numinous that the charismatic leader seems to live and breathe so effortlessly. By its nature charisma is not a continuous institution, and its authority (power) is inherently unstable and fleeting. For this reason, once the charismatic leaves the scene, it becomes more difficult to link the sacred qualities of the numinous with the power of the religious community.

Meanwhile, the social order of the religious group changes, evolves, becomes stabilized, never, however, without some experience of revolution prompted at the beginning by the holiness of the charismatic leader. In its most potent form, charisma disrupts rational rule and the current ideas of sanctity. The sacred traditions of the past are uprooted to make way for new ideas that speak directly for the numinous or divine and lead inevitably to new traditions as if sacralizing this current revolutionary force in history.

The rarity and short-lived experience of charisma forces us to soberly regard this phenomenon as unavoidably set on a course from the turbulently exciting life of closeness to the numinous, that knows no economic goals or rationality, to a slow death by suffocation under the weight of social need for routinization in the name of concrete and material goals.

The bureaucratic authority as we see it in Western Christianity today is our basis for comparison with the activity of charisma down through the centuries. The rational regulation arising from institutionalization calls the antagonistic forces of traditional authority and charismatic authority to a merger. Beyond mere rational regulation, both tradition and charisma share a loyalty to its leader and acknowledge the sanctity that flows from the numinous through the gifts of the leader. As these two forces merge, power in religious society becomes more keenly recognized in itself, but the task of ascertaining its roots in the sacred remains.

Conclusions

1) Power is basic to the understanding of life. Consequently, power is basic to the understanding of religion. At first, all power is impersonal. When it begins to touch us personally and we react, we are thrown into a new experience of relating

to power. Weber, in contrast to Otto and Van der Leeuw, places much emphasis on how we relate to the power of the numinous.

2) The idea of *Taboo* helps to link the concept of power to the concept of holiness. Once we regard some powerful object as exceptional, deserving of awe, we draw its meaning into the realm of the sacred.

3) The entire discussion of power and holiness cannot be approached as a simple rational endeavor. The value of a non-rational approach to the numinous is critical. (Nonrational in effect means supra-rational.) The supra-rational is more profound than the rational in approaching the numinous, but its ambit and ambiance are dreadfully elusive.

4) Numen as a term primarily emphasizes the idea of religious value not moral value. We call the numen august and shrink in humility, not because we are sinful, but because we are profane. Ultimately we learn of the numen as holy and powerful when we develop a sense of closeness to the numen. This closeness, curiously enough, is achieved on a supra-rational plane.

5) To understand holiness in our society today we must understand Weber's idea of charisma. Charism, to become legitimate, must have the subjective response of her followers. (Usually the holiness of a religious leader draws followers, although a power is implied.)

6) In the usage of Otto and Van der Leeuw Weber sees power in society as domination. He distinguishes power by itself which needs no acceptance and domination that calls for a measure of voluntary compliance. The legitimacy of domination implies the give and take between authority and subject. Thus, holiness and power are always being tested in society for legitimacy as social expressions of religion.

7) In recent times, society wants a rational tied-down legal approach to authority that shows power and promotes holiness. Yet, the legal-rational structure is not consistently effective in showing itself as endowed with the power and holiness of the numinous. Weber shows that the tradition and the charismatic uprooting of tradition are the two effective authorities for manifesting the numinous as power and holiness. In traditional authority and charismatic authority, awareness of power and holiness of the numinous come from a supra-rational sensitivity to the traditions and to the charisma. When an organized group chooses to subject itself to a charismatic authority, it is called a charismatic community. This response is predominantly supra-rational and emotional. (In Christianity, the charismatic community evolved towards an hierarchy between the second and fourth centuries.) While we strive to give a rational explanation to religious phenomena, the supra-rational elements cannot be overlooked.

8) If response to a charismatic leader is necessary for legitimacy, response to routinized or institutionalized religion that replaces the charismatic must be consistently strong for normal legitimacy of order. The problem today is to recognize power and holiness as legitimately expressed through the institutional structures that exist of necessity to meet the needs of large numbers of followers. In reality, the holy cannot be made available on a routine basis as institutionalized religion attempts to do. The numinous is special, set apart from the ordinary or profane. The charismatic leader calls attention to the sacred much more correctly than any institutionalized form of religion. But charismatic leadership is rare, and short-lived, almost as a volcanic eruption of a majestic peak on our Pacific Rim. In its most potent form, charisma disrupts rational rule and current ideas of holiness. But, the numinous is best understood in the atmosphere of the charismatic. Is not a volcano best understood when it erupts?

Discussion Questions

Chapter Three

1) Describe promal power as it evolves in religion.

2) How does taboo link power to holiness?

3) Describe the polar ideas of sacred - profane, holy - sinful in Otto's thought.

4) Describe the three elements of the holy in Otto's thought.

5) Distinguish power and domination in Weber's thought.

6) Discuss how charism in Weber's writings develops and endures.

7) How is a charismatic leader revolutionary?

8) How does charism relate power to holiness?

Notes

1 G. Van der Leeuw, *Religion in Essence and Manifestation* (New York: Harper and Row, Publishers, 1963) I, 24.

2 *Ibid.*, p. 25.

3 *Ibid.*, p. 27.

4 *Ibid.*, p. 83.

5 *Ibid.*, p. 89.

6 *Ibid.*, p. 38.

7 *Ibid.*, p. 43.

8 Rudolf Otto, *The Idea of the Holy* (New York: Oxford University Press, 1923), pp. 11-49.

9 Van Der Leeuw, *op. cit.*, I. 157.

10 *Ibid.*, I. 75.

11 Otto, *op. cit.*, p. 25.

12 *Ibid.*, p. 38-40.

13 Max Weber, *Economy and Society*, edited by Guenther Roth and Claus Wittich (Berkeley: University of California Press, 1978), I, 31.

14 *Ibid.*, I, 53-54.

15 *Ibid.*, I, 213.

16 *Ibid.*, I, 241.

17 Karl Rahner *et al.*, editors, *Sacramentum Mundi* (New York: Herder and Herder, 1968), I, 283-84.

18 Weber, *op. cit.*, I, 244.

19 *Ibid.*, II, 1139.

20 *Ibid.*, II, 1113.

21 *Ibid.*, II, 1117.

Chapter Four

Individual Religion

PART A
FROM DESIRE, TO SATISFACTION, TO VALUE

Individual Religion

The task today, little different from the task of mankind through the centuries, is to find the place of religion in our communal and individual lives.

Gordon Allport in his book, *The Individual and His Religion*, directs his attention to the place of subjective religion in the structure of personality "whenever and wherever religion has such a place."[1] Sociologists and psychologists agree that the persistence of religion in a world that appears so secular is a puzzle and perhaps an embarrassment to the scholars of today. Quoting *Emerging Trends* (vol. 8, no. 2, February 1986) published by Princeton Religious Research Center, Roof and McKinney[2] show that in the U.S. in 1952 only 2% registered no religious preference, while in 1985 that figure rose to 9% of the survey group. While this rise calls for serious reflection, nevertheless the personal religious sentiments of Americans — whatever the fate of institutional religion may be — are very much alive and show promise of thriving in the years to come.

Religious Feeling

Is there a basic form of experience that is common to every religious feeling or sentiment? Allport would say no. Investigating Schleiermacher and Rudolf Otto's idea of religion we see both an affective and cognitive sense of dependence in religious feelings. Moreover, for Otto the experience of the amazing and fascinating "absolute" leads into the double sense of security and longing that typifies a Western view of religious experience. Consequently, many psychologists[3] would agree that there is no single and typical religious emotion. Rather there are widely divergent sets of experiences that focus on a religious object. What is important is habitual and intentional focusing on experience rather than on the nature of the experience that should interest the psychologist as he investigates religious feelings. In most of the religions of the world the whole gamut of feelings and emotions is involved. In effect, the unique experience of the individual is respected as the psychologist attempts to measure those elements that are accepted as religious.

The Role of Desire

All of life revolves around desire. Most desires are "items" in religion. Prayer, for example, is an expression of desire. There is nothing that man could desire that some individual man has not prayed for. Beyond the basic desires of food, water, and shelter is the haunting emotion of fear. Our human life is haunted by fear – fear of enemies, of nature, of sickness, poverty, ostracism, and most of all, of death. Of all the creatures on earth man alone knows that he will die. How do we cope? Often we turn to religion or religious symbols. Moreover, the reciprocal of fear is the desire for companionship. In most human beings the capacity to love is great and the desire for love insatiable. Allport, believes it is doubtful whether even the happiest of earthly lovers ever feel that they love or are loved enough.[4] A margin of yearning remains. And if death snatches the beloved from this world, the desire mounts. "A small child," states Allport, "in her bereavement nightly addresses her prayers to her dead mother."[5] Culture does not sanction this practice; it is not taught by the elders, but it was for her a spontaneous solution of an insupportable conflict. Her religious practice was prompted by her natural orphan hunger.

Generally, it is in the critical periods of life when desire is intense and religious consciousness is acute. Many persons act religiously only in moments of crisis; the rest of the time they move along comfortably if not godlessly, content to allow their religious sentiment to lie dormant. However, in a multitude of ways the religious sentiment of the individual brings to focus the complex motives and mingled desires of an unfulfilled life.

Although the individual is seldom aware of it, he approaches his "god" or "ultimate concern" in relation to his current needs. In India the Hindu youth receives from his teacher a name for "god." This name is suited to the ends, temperament, and capacity of the initiate. With Whitehead and the Hindus Allport agrees that in the last analysis "each person confronts his deity in solitude."[6] Each person's path through religion is distinct. Theological and ritualistic preferences will vary according to one's emotional thresholds, and one's tendency to express or inhibit feelings. However, as Strunk agrees "the roots of religion that lie in temperament are but poorly understood."[7]

Psychogenic Desires and Spiritual Values

Religion for the individual person is the flower of desire. To appreciate this reality Allport guides us through a discussion of basic desires that lead to satisfaction and thus he introduces us to the word VALUE that is so important in any discussion of religion.

Allport distinguishes viscerogenic desires and psychogenic desires. Viscerogenic desires are subjective and private, normally clamoring for objects that bring direct bodily satisfaction. Psychogenic desires by contrast are objectified, i.e., seeking objects outside ourselves such as goodness, truth and beauty. The inner restlessness that seeks satisfaction of this type is more complex than the specifically localized drives of the body. Moreover the psychogenic desires are more human in contrast to the more animal motivation of viscerogenic desires.

Desire seeks satisfaction. Allport reminds us that anything that gives satisfaction we call a "value."[8] Chronologically viscerogenic values precede psychogenic values. Furthermore, in time values become more generalized. In the psychogenic realm a particular act of justice will yield satisfaction because it conforms to an abstracted class of activities that constitute our sense of what is good or right. Gradually goodness, beauty, truth become broad categories. Always they exist outside of ourselves in a realm of reality that becomes more and more universalized. (Incidentally there are some psychogenic interests that are relatively self centered and not always socially desirable, e.g. desires for power and self expression.)

Let us return to the idea of value or that which gives satisfaction. As an infant grows he becomes aware of himself as a distinct conscious agent separate from other persons and objects outside himself. From the age of two onward Allport tells us "the most universal of all values resides in the keen sense of individuality which constantly demands self-expression. . . . Our organisms are so constructed that our personal life is the highest value that we ever know directly."[9] (Does this idea not tell us something about the tragedy of suicide?)

As I gradually come to value myself I value whatever respects and preserves the dignity and integrity of the human person. Eventually I realize that my neighbor has the same human value I have. I begin to respect that. My values grow to take in all mankind and eventually the supreme expression of personality itself - God. The Golden Rule, or Second Great Commandment of Christianity is a statement of the value I affirm.

Thus, the psychogenic interest in the integrity and dignity of my personality develops to embrace all human values tied to human living. I grow eager that no values should perish. Beauty, truth, and goodness specified in the individual human being become interconnected and universalized in the infinite deity or "ultimate concern."

The concept of value led Hoffding[10] to declare that all religion is motivated by the individual's desire to conserve value. The typical sociologist adds: "religion is nothing more than a value system."

Review Outline

Personal Religion - Arises From:

Desire

1) Each person has desires that seek fulfillment (In the shadows lurk our *fears.*)
    - Desire for security
    - Desire for love
    - Fear of sickness and death

2) Desires heighten at dramatic periods in life
    - Birth . . .   This period heightens
    - Marriage . . .   religious consciousness
    - Death . . .

3) Types of desires:

    Psychogenic { *Outside our bodies*
    beauty, truth, goodness developed

    Viscerogenic { *Related to our bodies*
    Earlier desires
    Bodily
    More undeveloped

4) *Desire* seeks *satisfaction*

Anything that gives satisfaction is a *value* $\begin{cases} \text{Psychogenic} \\ \text{Viscerogenic} \end{cases}$

a) Chronologically I first value self, then other persons, then all mankind, then the source of mankind (universal value)

5) Religion is *basically* a value system

Because:
a) It provides a sense of unity among all values
b) It points toward the highest values

PART B
VALUES RELATED TO MEANING

Affinity of Purpose, Meaning and Value

Gordon Allport among several psychologists emphasizes the purpose of mankind is not merely to preserve life but to make life meaningful and worth living. All purpose exists in the present, but it also carries with it a futurity and growth dimension. As such, purpose or meaning wishes to identify values that make sense to individuals and to the community at large.

Victor Frankl has challenged the purely erotic or aggressive motivation of human personality and has identified the will to meaning as the basic stuff of human life. Human life for Allport, Frankl and other psychologists is more than survival. In a more humourous fashion, the film *Survivors* points up the inhumane qualities of merely surviving. Human life without purpose or meaning is a waste. Religion is the one discipline that assists the personality directly in searching for authentic meaning and purpose. Abraham Maslow said:

> The human being needs a framework of values, a philosophy of life, a religion or religion-surrogate to live by, in about the same sense that he needs sunlight, calcium or love . . . We need a validated, usable system of human values that we can believe in and devote ourselves to (be willing to die for), because they are true rather than because we are exhorted "to believe and have faith."[11]

Where do we find values? Does value rest on mere individual judgment or does the community assist us in finding values?

Value like so many other words seems vague and difficult to define. Variation bathes in the sea of complexity when we discuss words like justice, reason, freedom and truth. Value is that type word. Ralph Barton Perry in his *General Theory of Value* tells us that in every value three elements come into play, the subject who has an interest (I), the object of the interest (O), and the relationship between them (R). "I" for example, is the interest the wine taster has for Washington State wines, "O" is the particular wine of Washington State that is tasted, and "R" is the stimulus-response pattern that binds the two together.[12] If we remove subjective consciousness from this world we have no objects of value. Value does not exist in a world devoid of awareness. Value in the sense intended by Perry may be defined as a relational property that exists in an object when someone is interested in the object. In economic terms we immediately think of supply and demand. So determined, values are "objectively relative," that is, they are properties of objects relative to our preferences as subjects. The poorest painting in the world possesses value if someone happens to like it.

If we apply the term "value" to religion we can appreciate how an individual or a community places a value on life with its total considerations. By viewing life in its totality an individual or a community expresses a religious attitude. Hence, a religious person according to sociologists is someone who has a value system. For Tillich authentic value translates into an ultimate concern. G. Van der Leeuw[13] traces our religious sense of value to the Greeks. The oldest Greek measure of value was the ox, the sacred sacrificial animal. The ox served as a tribute that must be paid to the deity. As such, the tribute was like money or "worth." The resulting sacrificial meal, in the course of which the meat was equally divided, became the germ of public financial administration. Later on coin replaced the sacrifice. The coin was "money" or tribute and due to its originating in the sphere of sacrifice, brought with it special power and special value. Religious value expanded to take in economic value. In both cases the community was directly involved. When I look at city centers in Europe and city centers in America, I see a remarkable contrast. In America skyscrapers replace churches as the dominant edifices. These huge pillars of concrete, glass and steel are named after their owners, who in reality are banking and insurance corporations. Religion in America yields to economics as a value with a driving power so strong some may see it as ultimate.

This power of worth or value (residing first in the sacrifice and later in the coin) shows itself as a process of giving. It includes the giver, or subject who gives, the sacrifice or object of value and the receiver or deity. Sacrifice in its origins is always a gift. Later on it proceeded to take on special value. It now is no longer considered merely homage to gods as such; it is an opening to the blessed source of gifts. As givers, we both give and we receive. In gift-giving it is not possible to say precisely who is the donor and who is the recipient. Both participate in the power that is being presented, and as such, neither the giver nor the receiver (even though one be a god) occupies the focal point of the action.

The verb to give (*dare* in the Latin) does not mean merely to dispose of some arbitrary object with a quite indefinite intention. The word *dare* means, rather, to place oneself in relation to and then to participate in the second person by means of the object, which is really not an object, but is a part of one's self as giver. "To give" means therefore to convey something of oneself to a strange being so that a bond may be forged. As Emerson says in his essay "Gifts," "The only gift is a portion of thyself." Consequently, giving is the flowing of the giver to the recipient. Strangely enough, giving demands a gift in return, because by the flowing action the recipient comes into the power of the giver. To "carry one's weight" in this flowing process the recipient becomes a donor. The giving sets up a flow or process back and forth between receiver and donor. The Indian tribes of North West America call this flow of giving and receiving a "potlatch." Two tribes or chiefs engage in a competition of prodigality, each trying to outdo the other in gift giving so as to experience heightened power by means of the process.

The entire process centers on the relationship of mortal to god, or giver to recipient. What has value is the relationship ("R"). In the past the meat of the sacrificial act was divided among the members of the community who act both as donor and recipient. The gift is critical as a value; however, the principal feature or value is not that someone should give or receive something, but that the stream of life should continue to flow. The gift as a communion sacrifice is transplanted into the midst of life demonstrating a power that moves between giver and recipient saying in effect - *do ut possis dare*, i.e., I give in order that you may be able to give. In all of life's activities we search for meaning and value. The process of living is always gift giving if our relationship to givers and receivers is authentic. While value originates in animal sacrifice it extends to all "meaningful" acts of human living. Ritual and worship provide constant poignant reminders in the community of the variety of values each person finds in living. Interestingly enough what the individual wishes to conserve depends on his own needs, and needs vary from one individual to another, from nation to nation, from age to age. When values progress and rise above mere self-interest the character of religious expression broadens. Values always confront the struggle for existence. When values are threatened a conserving agent is needed. Here is the place where religion enters the picture. When the border experiences of life occur – death, disease, illness, fear, deprivation, insecurity – religion is sought to estimate or restore values.

Pursuit of Meaning

In Max Weber's distinction science deals with problems of empirical causation; philosophy deals with problems of first causes; and religion with problems of adequate meaning. Throughout life we know that our community knowledge (i.e. science) cannot explain all events and objects. For those areas of fact and experience that avoid ready explanation such as tragedy, death, serious hurt, etc. we need to find some sort of answer in terms of total reality. The human person turns to religion and asks: "What does this mean?" Even a poet's clear recognition of mystery in nature calls for an explanation. Tennyson shares with us his poet's insight:

Flower in the crannied wall
I pluck you out of the crannies
I hold you here, root and all, in my hand,
Little flower - but if I would understand

> What you are, root and all, and all in all,
> I should know what God and man is.

To learn the meaning of a flower would consequently provide meaning for other more cosmic, more mysterious subjects touching our own personal daily life.

We have already discussed desire, satisfaction and values. Relatively speaking these have more emotional roots than the idea of meaning which easily fits in the cognitive category. However, in the human person religious feelings or actions are not separated and distinguished in emotional and cognitive divisions. The whole person has a religious feeling; the whole person discovers meaning in life through some reflective process which the behaver calls religious.

It follows that an individual's religious life must be viewed as "an indistinguishable blend of emotion and reason, of feeling and meaning."[14] For the sake of our further discussion we can say that the cognitive-affective fusion is able to be described by the word, sentiment, though its flavor suggests feeling more than meaning.

Emotion and thought and its parallel feeling and meaning, yearn for unification in the individual's life. The religions of the world seek to unify events, objects and person's lives in some reasonable explanation of reality. A given science or art accounts for one part of reality. Religion seeks to unify all these parts. However, let us not overstate the role of religion. Men and women have human longing, e.g. food, drink, shelter and beauty, truth, goodness. We long for satisfaction of these needs but religion as well as any science or activity will not directly satisfy these longings. The nature of the human species is such that he will not reach satisfaction in this life. (Let us not speculate about the afterlife.)

While the human spirit longs to have full beauty, truth and goodness, he accepts along the path of this quest a system that gives meaning and unity to reality. The religious quest arising from the individual person is either a search for unity and meaning in an incomprehensible world, or it extends naturally to the end point and seeks ultimately as a religious quest a full explanation and understanding of all reality.

Since each individual is distinct, each has his own emotional and intellectual set of difficulties in facing reality and seeking a certain level of understanding, and unity of reality. In brief, the requirements for meaning vary from person to person and the pursuit often has a religious flavor in it.

Review Outline

Values

Example

1) Subject = Wine Taster

   Object = Washington State Wines

   Relationship = Stimulus — response pattern
   ↳ (the value)

2) Subject = giver of gift

   Object = receiver of gift

   Relationship = ⬛Gift given
   ↳ (the value) ↓
                  = ancient religion = sacrifice of ox... to ...coin

   the relationship indentifies, unites, and preserves values

   Tillich asks   - What value is ultimate?

                  - For a Westerner with a Judeo-Christian
                    background - it is God!

Values + Meaning

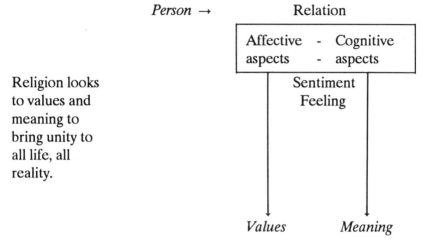

Religion looks
to values and
meaning to
bring unity to
all life, all
reality.

PART C
SCIENCE AND RELIGION

As we evolve in human living we clearly grow in our understanding of how science answers our questions and how religion is
called on to look to those questions that reach beyond empirical
verification. Take for example sickness and death. When we
summon a doctor and when we summon a priest we are acting on
entirely different levels. The doctor answers the questions: "Can
we heal or extend life in the face of this illness?" The priest answers the question: "Can we understand the reason for this person
moving towards death at this time and not at another, in this manner and not in another?" How a young child came to be burned to
death is an empirical question that can be answered on the scientific level. Why such a child should meet this tragic death is a question that goes beyond science. To face this latter question we move
to the area of religion.

Related to the cognitive problem of meaning are specific issues
that touch people's lives. Cosmological wonder linked to physical
and moral evil, the realization that we are the only animals that
know we will die are issues producing hope and optimism or sad-
ness and pessimism. As the Yogavasistha, a sacred Hindu text
states: "Let me know the best possible secret of becoming free
from the sufferings of life."[15]

The excitement of creation and the reality of evil in the creative
process are twin problems of meaning. Evolutionists like Chardin
and religious leaders down through the ages attempt to show the
unity of creation by linking growth and evil, as necessary experiences of this creative process. In any explanation the response is
directed to a religious request: ..."Tell me the meaning of life and
its puzzling and distressing circumstances." What religion does, is
provide some satisfactory framework or meaning and unity for life.
The result is hope and optimism but a very realistic hope that accepts pain and suffering as part of life.

All of our cognitive operations move toward coherence and unity. To accomplish this we seek categorical meanings and simplified explanations. The danger of course is to stereotype reality. Insofar as the religious quest seeks to explain the meaning and unity of all reality it runs the risk of categorization and simplification. However, insofar as religion constantly reflects on the continuing events of life and contrasts them with current views of universal meaning it has a better opportunity to face realistically the ambiguity of life that indicates some framework of unity.

The desire to live on is already an indicator of man's built in bias toward optimism. Hope springs eternal for the religious and seemingly less than religious person alike. The religious person simply wants to relate his hope to total reality and his personal experiences of suffering and hardship to the unity of the world.

Role of Culture

The threads of religion are lockstitches into the social and economic fabric of the community. A religion cannot be supplanted by another unless the basic culture is altered. A child brought up in an eastern tradition of religion may not understand it at first, but he will adhere to it as he grows insofar as he interiorizes the meaning system of the religion. Most of us in our mature years chose freely to remain in the religion of our culture. But then could we assume that religion can be defined in terms of culture? While we accept the general religious system of our culture and our parents we interiorize religion in a very personal and individualistic way. Few of us would mirror the precise religious views of our parents. But we do choose to retain many cultural and religious values taught to us in our youth.

All over the world on Sundays millions of Christians recite a common creed, but with innumerable shades of interpretation. Such variety does not weaken the historical faith of Christianity, but it does alert the social scientist and theologian to be aware of the individualism in religion as they pursue their science.

The conclusion of Gordon Allport is that the roots of religion are so numerous, the weight of its influence in individual lives so varied, and the forms of intellectual and emotional interpretation so endless that uniform religion is impossible. As personality develops and seeks out its higher expression it becomes more and more unique. Since no department of personality is subject to more complex development than the religious sentiment, it is in this area of human life that we must expect to find the widest divergences. With Allport we sense the impact of the title of William James' work: *The Varieties of Religious Experience.*

Review Outline

Meaning

- Science Looks to Causes

    e.g. Sickness

        Death and Life

- Philosophy Looks To First Causes

    e.g. Source of Sickness,

        Death and Life

- Religion Looks to *Meaning*

    - Why Should I Be Sick Now?

    - Why Should I Be Dying Now?

    Meaning
    └─Includes   *Me*   (My Experiences)

                      World   (World Experiences)

PART D
THE INDIVIDUAL RELATED TO THE COMMUNITY

RELIGION: COMMUNAL, UNIVERSALIZED, AND
INDIVIDUALIZED TOWARDS PERSONAL GROWTH

Two Questions

When we think of religion many of us picture in our minds a manifest community expression of religion in an act traditionally called worship. Meanwhile as we harbor a lingering memory of a "me - God" approach to religion so common in the recent past, two types of questions confront us:

1)   What is the role of the individual in religion? If an individual claims to have some sort of belief, but chooses not to express himself in a communal or social manner, is that individual still religious? In other words, must there be a social sharing of some of the traits found in religions so that some sort of agreement and support flows from this sharing?

2)   If an individual joins with other individuals in a community expression of religion, must this community of shared religious traits be institutionalized, i.e. be placed into a somewhat elaborate and enduring set of social relationships involving distinctions between leader and follower, between prophet, priest and layman? Admittedly, the line between social sharing and permanent institutions is not always easy to trace, but we do have existing religious institutions (e.g. Christianity) to use by way of example.

These two sets of questions will occupy our attention as we compare the notions of individual religiosity in the thought of Alfred North Whitehead, Thomas Luckmann and other leading sociologists and theologians. These questions are particularly important today when sectors of institutionalized religion are lamenting the decline. Words like secularization and desacralization are used in an attempt to explain the situation when actually a clear analysis of the problem is wanting.

In trying to determine the position of individual religious expression in our contemporary secularized world we must reflect upon several sociological and theological factors. In any sociological theory of religion, we must recall the distinction between individual existence and the social order. Both Max Weber and Emile Durkheim recognized that the problem of individual existence in society is a "religious" problem. If we are trying to determine the effect of secularization on the world we cannot look simply to external society, but we must determine the position of the individual as well.

Beginning with the Second World War and accelerating in the last decade the sociology of religion developed into a flourishing enterprise. Unfortunately the external growth of the science has not been accompanied by theoretical progress. The key authorities in the field have often been passed over. If men like Rudolf Otto, G. Van der Leeuw, Mircea Eliade, Roger Caillois, Joachim Wach and others were sufficiently understood, the current trend toward triviality would cease.[16] Two of the authorities, Max Weber and Emile Durkheim, saw religion as a key to the understanding of society. However, as time went on the goals of the sociology of religion narrowed, so that all that resulted was a description of the decline of ecclesiastical institutions — from the parochial viewpoint at that. Meanwhile its most significant task remains: the analysis of the changing social — not necessarily institutional — basis of religion in modern society. To arrive at this analysis the problem of personal religious expression in society must be faced.

What astounds Thomas Luckmann[17] is the complete failure in American sociology to recognize E. Durkheim's and George H. Mead's theory of the social origin of self. Both bring about a complete reversal of the traditional understanding of the relation between society and the individual. While in the past the individual had been generally viewed as the basic given element combining with other individuals to form society, Durkheim and Mead turn 180 degrees and posit society as the given element finding in it the needed conditions for individuation and the emergence of self. In the light of this reversal the understanding between religion, society and the individual person is yet to be articulated.

Whitehead's Idea of Religion

Alfred North Whitehead tells us: "in some sense or other, justification is the basis of all religion. Your character is developed according to your faith."[18] Whitehead reminds us that character and conduct in life depend on a person's internal conviction. These convictions are the basis of all religion. Expanding on this idea Whitehead notes that life is an "internal fact for its own sake, before it is an external fact relating itself to others."[19] Admittedly environment plays a major role in each of our lives but in whatever way we conduct ourselves externally it is the internal life initially that provides a basis for that conduct. "Religion" according to Whitehead, "is the art and theory of the internal life of man so far as it depends on the man himself and in what is permanent in the nature of things."[20] This description is a direct denial of the sociologists' theory that religion is primarily a social phenomenon.[21] Whitehead, however is ready to admit that we cannot separate society from man since man is both social and individual. But the collective emotions of man in society can leave unnoticed the awesome ultimate fact, which is the human being.[22] Consequently, "religion" for Whitehead, "is what the individual does with his own solitariness."[23] If a person is never solitary, he is never religious. Indeed by being caught in the rush of activities the typical contemporary person may be engaged in a very dehumanizing experience. Not to take time to be alone and to reflect is not only less than human, it is irreligious. Collective institutions, revivals, rituals, churches, codes and doctrines are the trappings of religion and flow from religious expression in a community. They can be useful or harmful, authoritatively determined or mere temporary expedients, but the goal of religion is beyond this. What should emerge from religion is individual worth of character. Again this worth can be good or bad, positive or negative. The important thing to notice in religion is its transcendent quality which can be appreciated most objectively by appealing to history.

Four Historical Factors

With gradual quickening in religious importance four factors are externalized in human history: ritual, emotion, belief and rationalization. Each stage dawns gradually in history. First ritual stands in isolation, then emotion takes the lead. Belief follows as explanatory of the complex of ritual and emotion, and eventually in its expression we recognize the germ of rationalization. Once belief and rationalization are established in religious history solitariness becomes discernible as constituting the heart of religion.[24]

Ritual and Emotion

Whitehead defines ritual as "the habitual performance of definite actions which have no direct relevance to the preservation of the physical organisms of the actors."[25] From superfluous energy and leisure man repeats the actions common for maintaining life (e.g. hunting and food gathering) for the sake of repetition. This exercise evokes joy and the emotion of success. As rituals develop so also do man's artistic tendencies. Emotions are excited for their own sake apart from biological reaction. The unintended effect is a sensitizing of the human organism for life beyond common work. Mankind through ritual embarks upon the adventure of feeling, emotion and ultimately play. Even today in our modern world religion evokes kindred notions in the words holy day and holiday.[26]

Belief and Rationalism

Paul Pruyser relates how the original emphasis was on ritual doing long before reflective thought about the meanings of the ritual occurred. As recently as the Reformation we recognized an emphasis on functional religion – preaching, singing, teaching – not simply thinking about God or religion. E. S. Ames likewise holds that feasts were celebrated, temples were built, and ceremonies flourished long before inquiries were made concerning their efficacy and long before the nature of their gods were questioned.[27]

However, ritual and emotion cannot long remain isolated from intellectuality. Religion in its further stages provokes thought and reflection. It causes the construction of concepts of things beyond immediate perception. In broken and uncoordinated fashion beliefs arise. At this point religion ceases to be merely social and attracts the individual person in his own reflective solitude. With the writing of the Bible we see the most vivid account of the entrance of rationalism into religion.

Originally relevant in the area between the Tigris and the Nile, the Bible shows the progressive solitariness of the religious idea. First, types of thought arise, then protesting prophets, isolated figures stirring the Jewish conscience, then one man with twelve disciples meeting almost complete social rejection, finally, the adoption for popular consumption of this man's doctrine by evangelists. We in the Western world have come to respect this chronology called the Bible as a basis for our own rational view of religion. In this fourth stage, "rational Religion," declares Whitehead, "is religion whose beliefs and rituals have been reorganized with the aim of making it the central element in a coherent ordering of life."[28] As general history attests, rational religion emerges from pre-existing religious forms conditioned by the general progress of the peoples in which it arose. With the development of human consciousness and ethical intuitions ideas become stabilized in society in recognizable forms of expression. Once this atmosphere is established ideas about religion can emerge. As Whitehead remarks, "You can only speak of mercy among a people who, in some respects are already merciful."[29]

Language itself is a reminder of our recently acquired ability to share ideas. It is only during a comparatively recent period of human history that there has existed any language with an adequate stock of general terms. Thus, the free exchange of general ideas is a late acquisition demonstrating how language and society grow together.

Like other institutions, within a thousand years of the Christian era religion was touched by rational criticism. The prophet Hosea ascribes to God: "For I desired mercy, and not sacrifice; and the knowledge of God more than burnt offerings." (Osee 6/6). Individual criticism confronts tribal custom; social expression yields to individualistic forms.

Individual experience of the progress of travel by the time Rome was at her height of power allowed tribal religion to move toward a more individualistic experience. When a tribe travelled it protected its tribal unity in the sifting of new ideas, but when an individual travelled he broke out of his own social structure and met strangers in terms of kindliness. When he returned home he promoted the habit of thinking dispassionately beyond the tribe. This process of individual travel began to build a world-consciousness (as contrasted with social-consciousness that nourished sensitivity to people already known and loved individually). In social consciousness thinking and acting are mixed with the notion of preservation. With the emergence of world-consciousness, the essential rightness of things is sought. The individual is indifferent; thinking is more objective. The concept of the goodness of God replaced the former emphasis in communal religion on the will of God. A. N. Whitehead states: "In a communal religion you study the will of God in order that He preserve you; in a purified religion, rationalized under the influence of a world-concept, you study his goodness in order to be like him."[30] Thus it is Whitehead's contention that communal religion evolves to individualistic religion with its rational perspective expanded to the scope of world-consciousness.

With the development of communal religion the individual stands out as one more reflective, more aware of the world in which he lives. The tribal or social religious consciousness connected to immediate surroundings moves out into the world towards universal consciousness. This endeavor to make the whole world intelligible is the work of the solitary thinker. Thus communal religion as it becomes universalized becomes individualized.

The relationship between universality and solitariness is based on the fact that universality is a disconnection from immediate surroundings.[31] The individual experiences the same detachment in his own quest for unity and intelligibility of reality. In this development of religion we can better understand what Whitehead means when he says, "Religion is what the individual does with his solitariness."[32] Although tribal religion is authentic, as it expresses itself in ritual and emotion, it remains incomplete.

Recalling the principle that reasoning is originally a solitary act, and consequently religion in its rational development is what a person does in his own solitariness, Whitehead identifies three allied concepts to support his understanding of religion. These concepts are:

1) That of the value of an individual for itself.

2) That of the value of the diverse individuals of the world for each other.

3) That of the value of the objective world which is a community derivative from the interrelations of its component individuals and also necessary for the existence of each of these individuals.[33]

Religious consciousness begins with self-valuation, but it broadens into the concept of the world as a realm of adjusted values. Man in his own solitude asks: "What is the way of value?" He finds it by entering into the world as a full human being. This movement into the world as a full human being is a religious expression, for "religion," as Whitehead reminds us, "is world-loyalty."[34] At this point we notice Whitehead's acceptance of a communal expression of religion developing from an already solid individual expression in its rational aspects. The question of community today is tied to the judgment of one rational expression (individual religiosity) compared with the other (communal religiosity). Should a person today practice religion in solitude or join a community of believers?

Once we accept the rational development of religion in the human person we are asking a new question, namely; How can a believing community assist an individual who already embraces rational religion?

Individual and Communal in Relation

Relationship is basic to all of Whitehead's thought. He sees the universe as thoroughly interdependent. The body influences the mind; the mind influences the body. Physical energy encourages zeal; zeal conversely stimulates the body. The individual forms society; society in turn forms the individual. Accepting these principles compatible in sociology and philosophy Whitehead opens the way for recognizing the tension of individual and communal expressions of rational religion when he says:

> The actual world, the world of experiencing and of thinking, and of physical activity, is a community of many diverse entities; and these entities contribute to, or derogate from the common value of the total community. At the same time, these actual entities are, for themselves, their own value, individual and separable. They add to the common stock and yet they suffer alone. The world is a scene of solitariness in community.
>
> The individuality of entities is just as important as their community. The topic of religion is individuality in community.[35]

Religious expression, particularly through doctrine, is a return from solitariness to society. Whitehead looks to the person as subject and reminds us that there is no such thing as absolute solitariness.[36] Each person requires an environment. No man can isolate himself from society. As the individual certifies himself outward expression is necessary. As social, the human person confirms his individual conviction in the objective world where it will be tested and shared. The Christian Gospel, or Good News, is a clear example of individual conviction moving toward universality.[37] Religious truth first expressed in response to an individual experience undergoes formulation into precise doctrines or dogmas for a community and then yields to the transformation of history and traditions. If we recognize the idea of relationship as pivotal to Whitehead's thought we can accept the possibility of harmonizing Whitehead with sociologists like J. Milton Yinger. A complete religion for Yinger is a social phenomenon[38] while Whitehead sees religion as "individuality in community."[39] Insofar as Whitehead ably delineates the relationship of individual and social his explanation is more attractive. Yinger by contrast moves strongly to an emphasis on the social aspects of religion. He says that both the feelings from which religion springs and the "solutions" it offers are social; they arise from the fact that man is a communal or social animal. The "ultimate" questions identified as the center of the religious quest are ultimate primarily because of their impact on human association. Even death is not fundamentally an individual crisis, but a group crisis, threatening to tear the fabric of family and community. Yinger finds support in Joachim Wach (*The Comparative Study of Religion*) who holds that all religions, despite their wide variations, are characterized by three universal expressions: the theoretical, or a system of beliefs, the practical, a system of worship, and the sociological, a system of social relationship. Unless all of these are evident, one may have religious tendencies, religious elements, but not a full religion.[40]

Nonetheless Yinger like Whitehead attempts to keep the distinction between individual and communal in focus. Yinger says that it is a matter of empirical observation that most, if not all, odd religions combine group and individual elements. They are generally concerned with both individual salvation and group integration. This dual reference may derive from the fact that each of these functions of religion is carried on more effectively within a religious system that contains the other also. Individual needs may be more adequately met by a shared system of beliefs, by a religion that furnishes some measure of the integration of society necessary for individual life. And the group functions may be adequately performed only by a religious system that seems to satisfy at least some measure of the needs of individual adherents. Unfortunately, the various functions will not always be found together within a single religious tradition.

Bronislaw Malinowski likewise contends that religion needs the community as a whole so that its members may worship in common its sacred things and its divinities, and society needs religion for the maintenance of moral laws and order. In primitive religion this occurred in the identification of the whole tribe as a social unit with its religion. While Durkheim maintains that religion is social for all its entities, yet according to Malinowski anyone who had experienced religion deeply knows that the strongest moments come in solitude, in turning away from the world, in mental detachment, and not in distraction in a crowd. Malinowski asks, "Can primitive religion be so entirely devoid of the inspiration to solitude?"[41] For Malinowski moral attitudes related to religion work in the individual through the forces of the individual mind. From an ethical viewpoint primitive religion is neither exclusively social nor individual but a mixture of both. Hence, contrary to Durkheim, Malinowski agrees with Whitehead as he reflects that religion in primitive societies arises to a great extent from purely individual sources.

However, in primitive religion social co-operation is needed to surround the unveiling of things sacred with solemn grandeur. The community wholeheartedly engaged in performing the forms of the ritual creates the atmosphere of homogeneous belief. In this collective action those who least need the comfort of belief help those who are most in need of it. Moreover, the transmissions and conservation of sacred tradition entails publicity or at least collectiveness of performance.[42] Basically Malinowski wants to give due credit to both the individual and social elements in primitive religion. Lest we think our problems today regarding individual religiosity are unique, we see in Malinowski's study the emerging critical awareness of both the individual and social concepts of religion.

David L. Edwards in *Religion and Change* likewise supports Whitehead's view of the individual in the concept of religion. Edwards contends: "Man's basic religious sense may be interpreted largely through the faith of the surrounding society; yet it is, after all, the individual who makes the interpretation and — specially when his society is disintegrated — the individual is liable to be concerned with questions which go deeper than his place in soci-

ety."[43]   This understanding of the individual is most important today because of the individual's freedom and autonomy in a secularized world. According to Edwards secularization occurs when
supernatural religion, i.e. religion based on belief in God or a future state, becomes private, optional and problematic.[44]   Later on
in his study he admits however that the spectacles with which a religious believer (or an atheist) views reality are usually spectacles
provided by his society.[45]

	Carl Gustav Jung and his followers view religion both as a cul-
tural product and as an experience which at once integrates the
personality and unites the individual with society in its traditional
values.[46]   For Jung religion indeed is that force that gives meaning
to life.

	In support of Jung, Glen M. Vernon says: "It is almost impossible
to dissociate the individual from the groups to which he belongs
except for analytical purposes . . . the individual and society are
twin born and twin bred."[47] By way of further explanation he adds:

> As the sociologist views it, culture is to the group what personality is to the
> individual ... Culture is composed of the behavior patterns of the group.
> Personality is made up of the behavior patterns of the individual, (most of
> which occur in a group). Culture is learned; personality is similarly learned.
> Culture includes religion. Personality includes religion.[48]

The appreciation of the individual's role in religion has been different for Protestants from that experienced by Roman Catholics.
A major element in Protestant theology and ethics has been the
emphasis on individualism, In the broad stream of Protestant
teaching, from its beginnings, every man was felt to be the judge of
his own religious convictions. Protestantism indicated that the individual could establish direct personal (individual) contact with his
God. Protestants talked of the priesthood of all believers, who had
the liberty and the competence to come into the presence of God
without a special priest or intermediary, so that each might determine, either by himself or in consultation with his friends, the will
of God. Roman Catholic teachings have not stressed individualism
so strongly as Protestantism. Roman Catholics have shown greater

emphasis on group ritual. Often in the past there was the stress on approaching God through an intermediary such as Mary, or a great saint, who it was believed would intercede with God on behalf of the believers.[49] Rem Edwards[50] points out that social sharing was of the utmost importance in early Christianity. Paul insists, "You are members of one another." Edwards reflects that recent sociological studies indicate that it is extremely difficult for a set of religious beliefs, practices, and values to survive for very long under conditions of complete social isolation.

Organized Religion

Another inadequacy that has surfaced in the recent sociology of religion is its assumption that church and religion can be identified. What occurs is an open admission of giving in to narrowness by asserting that religion may be many things but it is amenable to scientific analysis only to the extent that it becomes organized and institutionalized.[51] In effect religion becomes a social fact either as ritual (institutionalized religious conduct) or doctrine (institutionalized religious ideas). In the absence of a well-established theory of religion this externalized and isolated view allows secularization to be regarded simply as a process of religious pathology measured by the shrinking influence of the institutional churches. Once the identity of church and religion is allowed, any explanation of religion today in terms of the individual remains scientifically inadequate. The desire to "measure" or evaluate religiosity is admirable, but a procedure that looks only to the institutional doctrines is hardly acceptable. Thus a true sociology of religion cannot be converted to a narrowly conceived "sociography" of the churches even if the patrons of the study are the church representatives themselves.

While church-oriented religion constitutes only one and perhaps not even the most important element in the picture that characterizes religion in modern society, it would be foolish to disregard the abundant data which recent research related to church-oriented religion in contemporary industrial societies has provided.

For example, from research we learn that in the United States religion has a broad middle-class distribution. Admitting that no simple unilinear and one-dimensional theory of secularization can be maintained, we are finding that the trend toward secularization in the U.S. is more the result of a radical inner change in American church religion than anything else.[52] According to Thomas Luckmann the change consists in the adoption of the "worldly" or "secular" version of the Protestant ethos through a unique constellation of factors in American social and religious history.[53] At least the data from one limited investigation of the sociology of religion alerts us to the alteration in two areas of focus in the present process of secularization:

    a) the social location of church religion, and

    b) its inner universe of meaning.

While it would be interesting to learn the causes that pushed traditional church religion to the periphery of modern society it seems more valuable to ask whether anything called "religion" in the framework of sociological analysis has replaced traditional church religion in modern society. This latter question forces us to look for individual and social expressions of religion not necessarily tied to church-oriented religion.

In looking further into the causes of secularization we see at least an indirect relation between industrialization, urbanization, and the transformation in the pattern of individual life in society. Originally the values underlying church religion were not institutional norms but norms socially lending significance to individual life in its totality.[54] With industrialization and urbanization a tendency arose towards institutional specialization which shrunk the base of specialized religious institutions. Eventually values institutionalized in church religion yielded to an integration and legitimation of values for every day modern life. Thus the shrinking of church religion as such does not alarm us. We simply must proceed further to ask what are the dominant values overarching contemporary culture and what is the social and religious basis of these values.

Experience of Self

In order to discuss an individual expression of religion we should first ask how anyone can estimate the authenticity of one's own experience. Immediately we shall note the sociological principle that results from this question, namely: that the individuation of consciousness is a possibility realized only in the social process.[55] To achieve the proper detachment and objectivity in viewing one's personal experiences we look to our fellow men and begin to share in his experiences. Once we participate with our neighbor in objective events and situations mediated in space and time we have the possibility of someone else observing the shared situation. Thus we share in the subjective processes of our fellowmen and test them against our own impressions of the same event. The result is a certain detachment and objectivity gained by both parties. What we are doing is importing an external and objective point of view for a subjective experience. This can only occur in the reciprocal social process of a face-to-face situation. In effect, this detachment from an immediate experience produced by a confrontation with our fellow man leads to the individuation of consciousness and permits the individual to build interpretative schemes in relation to past, present, and future. Ultimately the individual person can build systems of meaning.

Continuous social relationships allow the person to transcend his biological nature and become a self, i.e. becoming one who has successfully embarked upon the construction of an "objective" universe of meaning. To Luckmann this whole social process leading to the formation of self is fundamentally religious because it is the basis for the historically differentiated social forms of religion.[56]

We recall that the construction of meaning systems rests on detachment and integration presupposing a face-to-face encounter of individuals participating in the social process. We further note that the organism becomes a self by constructing with others an objective and moral universe of meaning. In this experience the organism transcends its biological nature. Thomas Luckmann feels justified in calling this process fundamentally religious.[57] Presently we may consider Luckmann's conclusion as valid in respect to the nature and activity of man as a self considered on the anthropological level. Meanwhile history reminds us that meaning systems have been constructed generation after generation so that man enters into society with rather sophisticated meaning systems already in existence. What does contemporary man do? Rather than attempting to construct "meaning systems" from scratch, man transcends his own biological nature by internalizing an historically "established" or given universe of meaning. The human being thus becomes a self in this concrete process of socialization.

In terms of the single human organism, both Whitehead and Luckmann would agree that the process of becoming a self, or transcending one's biological nature is fundamentally religious. In terms of socialization, in which personal transcendence is achieved, the process is likewise considered to be fundamentally religious. Both of the above are aspects of the universal anthropological condition of religion. The individual consciousness is actualized in the social processes. This is shown historically with the build up of adequate terms and symbols. Eventually, a "universal meaning" or world view exists in the developing community. When the individual internalizes this world view he recognizes several ways in which this view transcends himself as an individual. The very fact that the world view is socially objectivated and established in history helps us to understand its function for the individual. What is deeply appreciated is the opportunity to draw upon an existing reservoir of meaning rather than being faced with the problem of constructing a basic system of meaning from scratch. By being socially accepted or objectivated the world view recorded in history asserts a definite base of stability. As a result, the historical priority of a world view established by society provides the empirical basis for the successful transcendence of the biological nature of human organisms.[58] The world view in itself performs a religious function which is seized by society in the socialization process but primarily by the individual in becoming a self in the same process. This "world view" as an elementary social form of religion becomes a stepping off point for an investigation of religiosity today outside the institutional structures.

Nature of World View or World Consciousness

The world view could be described as an encompassing system of meaning for all socially relevant categories of reality. In connection with this, we note that socialization is the process by which the world is objectivated. This social process by which the world view is objectivated in society captures our attention so that we can anticipate the possibilities of personal religiosity in a community. While some forms of objectivation are represented by symbols such as flags, icons, or totems, the most significant form in which a "world view" becomes objectivated is language. When man acts in society we can consider this act as individual or social, depending on the internal spirit of the act. The problem always exists of finding out what is subjectively meaningful to the individual in responding to norms that are imposed from without. To sociologists like Luckmann and Peter Berger[59] language is the most important objectification of the world view, because it contains the most comprehensive system of interpretation. This system can be internalized by any individual member of society and all experiences of all members can be potentially located within the system.

The world view has a reservoir of model solutions and procedures for solving problems, which most distinctly is shown through the mediation of language. However, if the world view is the elementary form of religion as an encompassing system of meaning for reality today, we must remember that on various levels there should be all sorts of schemes and recipes for understanding this world view. No single interpretive scheme performs a religious function in itself. Rather it is the world view as a whole, as a unitive matrix of meaning, that provides historically the context within which human organisms identify as selves and transcend their biological nature. Thus the world view as a social form of religion (respecting individual and community) is both elementary and non-specific.[60] It is non-specific because it stands in a dialectic relationship with the social structure as a whole. At this point, we ask what additional distinct forms of religion may be shown in society and how are they related to the elementary and non-specific objectivation of religion in the world view.

We repeat once again that the world view as a whole performs a religious function, and no single element of the world view is to be designated as religious. However, Luckmann qualifies that statement. He says that symbols can portray a certain trait of the world view as a whole and insofar as they are symbolic and participate in the world view these individual symbols could be called religious.[61]

Arranged in a hierarchy of significance from typifications of the world of everyday life (e.g., walking, eating, running) to higher level of reflective models (e.g., slogans, proverbs) that become more concrete and more imposing on the life of the community, these symbols of religiosity show that the hierarchy of significance remains a "structural" trait of the world view. Thus, events of everyday life make sense in graduated strata of meaning and have value insofar as they relate to the world view which in itself is non-specific. As men reflect on certain events that transcend the world of everyday life, they label these events or qualities as sacred. If the quality of everyday life is profaneness, the quality that describes the transcendent area of life is its sacredness. Hence, both the ultimate significance of everyday life, participation in the world view, and the meaning of "different" or "transcendent" experiences are located in a sacred area of reality.

Review Outline

PERSONAL GROWTH

Desire to Find Self

- How? I Must Transcend My Biological Nature

- (Basic To Finding Social Meaning System)

The Entire Process *Therefore* Is Religious As Rooted In Search For *Meaning*

Desire To Find Universal Meaning (Same As World View)

- Meaning Systems Are Handed Down By Society

  - Through Language

- Personal Decision To Accept Existing Meaning Systems Or to Develop A Variation On The Existing Meaning Systems Is Part of Growth.

PART E
BUILDING A WORLD VIEW

THE SACRED AND PROFANE IN MOVEMENT
AND CONTRAST

Three Areas of the Sacred

The deepest religious experiences in society are those connected with birth, marriage and death - "the crises of existence" - as they are called.[62] Every religion we know has based itself in some degree on human social needs and aspirations. We usually think of religion, at least Western religion, as looking to the supernatural when actually, in our experience of religion in society, the deepest roots of religion lie in this earth with every day life. Successful religion traditionally has had a deep impact on the estranged, the alienated, and the socially or spiritually disinherited. Why? Whether or not religion promotes ritual, ceremony, priesthood and belief in the afterlife, religion always has a sense of the sacred shared in the community. This sense according to Durkheim goes to the very roots of religion.

Once again we state that the most basic elements of the kinship community were rites dealing with birth, marriage, and death. Starting with our experience of birth we reflect that no one in the ancient family system or even in many family systems existing today was literally born into his family. The biological fact placed the infant in the home, but until the infant was baptized or given formal entry into the family through ritual that could appease the souls of the departed and would confer on the newborn proper kinship identity he or she was not really "born." The ritual occurring several days after biological birth, through which the child was accepted into the family or religious community of the family, was the "birth" that counted.

Moreover, it was the family's right exercised through its head and often after consultation with the elders, to reject the infant, to put it to death as painlessly as possible, if it was not physically normal, or if demand on the available food supply made any new mouths a threat to the community's well being.[63] Consequently, birth was the first of the crises of existence that had to be met through sacred means. The social identity given to the infant through the ritual became the foundation of the sanctity of human life within the community. This ritual expression of sanctity of life continues in various ways down to our present time.

Marriage was the next significant stage in a kinship community, and in the religious community established within it. In the ancient kinship systems, such as that of the Greeks, Romans and Persians, marriage in itself did not establish a new family or household. Marriage was not like a contract uniting two distinct people - man and woman. Rather, like the birth rite, marriage was a means whereby the female was adopted into the family of the male to become a legitimate mate for the male. When the young woman moved into the household of her mate, she abandoned her father's religion and adopted the religion of the new household to which she became attached.

Death likewise was an integral part of this kinship religion. Death rites were most important because it was only through the small amounts of food left on the hearth at night that the souls of the departed members of the family were sustained in the afterlife.[64]

In the ancient Roman family reverence for the dead in no way resembled the Christian reverence for the saints. One of the main rules of Roman religion was that reverence or "worship" could be offered by each family only to those deceased persons who belonged to it by blood. The law forbad a stranger to approach the tomb. This reverence for the dead really was nothing more than reverence for ancestors. Sadly, a person who died childless received no offerings and was exposed to perpetual hunger. Far worse, a person who died childless, lost his identity after death. Without children this identity of a departed ancestor would be forever lost. Wealthy Romans erected tombs for themselves on highways such as the "Via Appia Antica" to insure that they would be remembered in the afterlife - if only by the passers by. When Christianity came to the Roman culture via Peter and Paul, the Romans saw this new religion as a great social force as well as an aid to personal spirituality. The respect for birth, marriage and death was renewed and invigorated in the customs of this modern religion.

In reviewing the various experiences in life we consider sacred, Luckmann urges us to see both the sacred and profane not as two separate poles, but as related in some manner in lesser or greater degrees of interpretation. If the world view is manifested in everyday life in some way that points up transcendence or sacredness, it is a religious reality.

When we look for meaning in everyday experiences or an indication of participation in a world view, we tend to exercise both logic and a pragmatic sense. Ritual acts, by contrast, embodying an element of the sacred cosmos are cognitionally meaningless in terms of everyday life but have their meaning in terms of the sacred cosmos. In all these expressions, language is the most important medium for the objectification of the world view. To build up a sense of the world view, concrete processes of socialization by means of specific religious representations or themes occur in the everyday life of society. These specific religious representations or themes are effective in shaping individual consciousness, not in themselves but in their position in the hierarchy of significance which these themes indirectly represent. Thomas Luckmann sums it up by saying:

> The hierarchy of significance which characterizes the world view as a whole and which is the basis of the religious function of the world view is articulated in a distinct superordinated layer of meaning within the world view. By means of symbolic representations that layer refers explicitly to a domain of reality that is set apart from the world of everyday life. This domain may be appropriately designated as a sacred cosmos. The symbols which represent the reality of the sacred cosmos may be termed religious representations because they perform in a specific and concentrated way the broad religious function of the world view as a whole. The world view in its totality was defined earlier as a universal and nonspecific social form of religion. Conse-

quently, the configuration of religious representations that form a *sacred universe* is to be defined as a *specific historical social form of* religion.[65]

When the individual is aware of a sacred cosmos in society he begins to reflect upon his life in relation to the role of the sacred cosmos. Basically the sacred cosmos is a social form of religion characterized by specifically segregated religious representations within the world view and therefore open to all individuals. There is no specialized institutional basis for these representations. However, as a matter of historical fact, the more complex society becomes the more likely it is to develop institutions to support the objectivity of the sacred cosmos. In our classical civilizations of the West, institutional specialization brought on institutionalized priesthood. In time individuals saw themselves as participants in a sacred cosmos or a world view *only* in terms of specialized institutional religion so that religion itself became identified with the institution. We can see the potential problem for a man today who considers himself irreligious because he does not join in the acts of any particular religious institution; yet, he may have a healthy world view and maturely reflect his identity or self in the experience of transcending his biological nature.

As an institutional priesthood emerges, greater is the likelihood that religious events or sacred events will become the charge of relatively specialized social roles. Likewise the more complex society becomes, the more heterogeneous is the social distribution of the world view and the more uneven becomes the distribution of religious representations. Thus, the integrating function of the sacred cosmos as a whole is threatened, for once religion is localized is special social institutions, an antithesis between religion and "society" develops.[66]

Thomas Luckmann delineates the position of the individual as he attempts to determine his expression of religiosity as follows:

Religion is rooted in a basic anthropological fact: the transcendence of biological nature by human organisms. The individual human potential for transcendence is realized, originally, in social processes that rest on the reciprocity of face-to-face situations. These processes lead to the construction of objec-

tive world views, the articulation of sacred universes and, under certain circumstances, to institutional specialization of religion. The social forms of religion are thus based on what is, in a certain sense, an individual religious
phenomenon: the individuation of consciousness and conscience in the matrix of human intersubjectivity.

The concrete historical individual, of course, does not go about constructing
world views and sacred universes. He is born into a pre-existing society and
into a prefabricated world view. He does not, therefore, achieve the status of
a human person in genuinely original acts of transcendence. Humanity, as a
reality that transcends biological nature, is pre-established for him in the social forms of religion. The individuation of consciousness and conscience of
historical individuals is objectively determined by historical religions in one of
their social forms.[67]

When man enters into the world he enters a process of socialization that gives him the opportunity to interiorize and internalize an
accepted historical "world view." His task is to take the objective
system of meaning and make it a part of himself While he may not
always be able to recognize it, he will follow a hierarchy of significance supporting the world view under a subjective system of relevance. Again, while the individual may not be able to explain readily in concrete terms what his subjective system of relevance is,
nevertheless, this system will be a constitutive element of his personal identity by virtue of the fact that it manifests itself consistently as a pattern of priorities in the individual choices of his daily
life. Thus, as man becomes conscious of his individual self he is accepting a world view already posited by society before him. In contrast to Whitehead's idea of the relationship of world consciousness
to individuality Luckmann defines the world view as a universal social form of religion while he defines personal identity as a universal form of individual religiosity.[68]

Sacred Cosmos and Institutions

How a person acts in the light of this world view brings us back
again to the term sacred cosmos, or that which by identifying its
"different" or "transcendent" experiences represents symbolically

the hierarchy of significance underlying the world view. Like the world view itself, the individual will internalize the sacred cosmos if it is a part of objective reality. He does this by specific religious representations. In this way the routine and the crises of individual life are placed into a transcendent context of meaning and are legitimated by the logic or "sense" of the sacred cosmos.

Review Outline

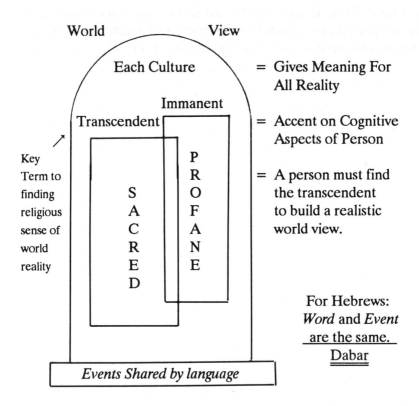

World View

Each Culture = Gives Meaning For All Reality

= Accent on Cognitive Aspects of Person

= A person must find the transcendent to build a realistic world view.

Immanent

Transcendent

Key Term to finding religious sense of world reality

SACRED

PROFANE

Events Shared by language

For Hebrews:
Word and *Event*
are the same.
Dabar

- No one manner of interpreting world view is religious but the search in general is religious.

- They symbols that open up the world view *become* religious, (e.g. Crossing the Red Sea, birth, marriage, death).

- Border issues (e.g. tragic death, famine, poverty, disease) must be explained in relation to world view.

- The change of experiences of the sacred, or the change in estimating what is sacred is called secularization.

PART F
RETURN TO THE CENTRAL QUESTION: THE INDIVIDUAL
RELIGIOUS PERSON IN THE COMMUNITY

THE INSTITUTIONAL CHURCH AND CHRISTIANITY

Historically there has been a great degree of institutional specialization of religion in the West. For this reason, religion traditionally has been mediated by the "church." The individual, attempting to express his religiosity finds often much to his chagrin
that his expressions are shaped directly by a historical church.
Within the institutional church those performances that are directly related to the sacred cosmos are fixed in doctrine and liturgy
which are interpreted by an official body of experts. In an investigation of secularization, the fact that individual religiosity is shaped
by highly specialized institutions has important consequences. The
chief consequence being that the individual begins to see his relationships to the world view or sacred cosmos only in terms of the
institutional structures. What makes the sacred stand out so
sharply from the profane is the way the sacred is interpreted by the
institution in matters of ultimate significance. As long as the institution offers a coherent model of reality, it will be followed. However, once that model loses its coherence, people will move apart
from the institution. Luckmann discusses three ways in which this
coherence is endangered:

1) One danger occurs when the official model of religion not
   only includes articulations of the sacred cosmos, but also interpretations of how individuals in the church must exercise
   their role in relation to the sacred cosmos and other social institutions.

2) The second danger occurs when the official model of religion
   is formulated as a set of highly specific norms for living and
   believing. One side effect is that the sacred cosmos becomes

more and more separated from the world of the believer and
as the role requirements of religion are fulfilled, religion becomes more and more routine.

3) The third danger involves the group of specialists
   implementing the official model of religion. As the experts
   become more tied to the role of interpreting the sacred
   cosmos, and to the theory and administration of the sacred
   institutions they become completely divorced from the typical
   routine and life experiences of the laymen. As a result, they
   are no longer able to serve the layman by presenting coherent
   models for religiosity.[69]

The Central Question

We return again to our central question: in what way do we understand the individual expression of religion?

Merely, by looking at research on church religion in industrial
societies we would find that religious expression is generally de-
clining. While Church religion transmits an "official" model of religion through the specialists or "experts" the more the institutional
Church tends to stabilize the model the more the gap grows between the "model" and the layman's evolving relationship to this
"model" of religious expression.

What can happen is that one official model is replaced by another model. If, however, the official model remains obligatory for
one segment of the population while another segment of the population embraces the new model, both models become less than official and pluralism begins to enter the picture. With this new-
found pluralism the autonomy of the individual is heightened. He
now makes choices in the internalization process of ultimate
meaning.

Thus at this point we might safely say that the norms of traditional religious institutions cannot serve as a yardstick for assessing
religious expression in contemporary society.[70] How much of an
influence institutional religion will have in the future is another

question. What interests us is the specification of individual religious expression for our time as it often shows itself outside the traditional institutional expressions of the community.

Institutions and Christianity

We are not trying to determine whether or not we should have institutions. Every human science accepts the need for institutions.[71] What we must ascertain is the role of institutions in religion, particularly the Christian religion we know in the Western world. In general, human institutions are erected to meet human needs. When people wish to accomplish a huge or difficult task they cannot achieve alone, they unite their energies with others and direct their efforts toward the common goal. Briefly this is what is understood by the term institution. Stemming from contractual rather than natural agreement institutions need not be dehumanizing. Ideally the institution strives for a goal which enhances rather than detracts from the humanizing process of individuals. Experience shows that institutions are necessary for any kind of human progress on the social, economic, political or religious level. Viewed sociologically the "Christian Church" (i.e. Christianity in all its denominations) is a unique institution insofar as it exists for and in Christ. Nevertheless there is a great amount of the human element in this institutional Church as specified in its own district institutions. Hence, the Church as institution can suffer all the problems of any other institution.

If institutions are considered necessary for human development, why do so many contemporary Christians shy away from the institutional Church? Kevin O'Rourke[72] offers two reasons: First, many Christian institutions (schools, churches, hospitals) have been conducted as though they were the only communities to which the individual Christian belongs. They were considered "total institutions" capable of fulfilling all human needs. Some of these institution were conducted in a manner that seemed to say: "The Christian exists for the institution and not the institution for the Christian." However, the sociologists remind us that the institution is a secondary group that is task oriented. By contrast it is the primary group (usually the family) where the basic personality growth is experienced. Primary groups aim at helping the individual grow both as a person and as a believer. The secondary group aims at tasks on a wider level of religious growth.

The second reason offered for contemporary Christians shying away from the institutional Church is that many of the "institutions" within the Church have not been renewed in the spirit of the international ecumenical movement (World Council of Churches) and Vatican II. Thus, it is possible that the individual Christian may receive adequate support from his primary group, but lacks support from the secondary group to the point of feeling separated.

In the 70's the "Jesus People" movement in the United States had demonstrated that young people seek out fellowship and authority in the institutional Church as a secondary group. Through their baptism young Christians witness to faith in Christ, but because confessional boundaries play no significant role in their life they seem to rebel against the institutional Church. By their actions they raise the practical question: Can I be a Christian without the Church? In other words they ask: Can I cling to Jesus by associating only with Christians in the primary group? Theologians such as Paul Wacker[73] declare that no road which bypasses the Christian Church leads a Christian to Jesus. The historical Jesus is available to Christians only by way of Kerygma. In the primitive Church the kerygma becomes the New Testament Scriptures, but always it is the preaching of the Christian community that brings Christ to potential believers. The faith of the preacher who responds to the world of God leads the potential believer to fellowship. Faith as a personal act involves the whole person saying "Yes" to Christ. He does not say "Yes" apart from the community. Moreover, the goals of Christianity call for support not only from primary groups but also from secondary groups (i.e. institutions) so that the Good News can be broadcast. An individual in society does not live merely in a family. He goes out into the wider world. The follower of Christ, who was a "man for others," lives his faith by going out to others. This activity of necessity enters the secondary groups making up the "institutional" Church. Christianity received its start from the Resurrection faith of the primitive Christian community. Without the post-Easter preaching the Good News of Jesus Christ would not have spread. Recent quests for the historical Jesus have demonstrated that the faith of the community certifies Jesus' historical mission. A Christian's salvation comes from both the historical cross of Jesus, and the Resurrection faith of the community recalling his preaching and ministry. By this Kerygma Jesus lives and is active in the community. Christianity is indeed a community experience hardly limited in origin and goals to primary groups.

When we think of primary and secondary groupings in Christianity, the appointment of the twelve apostles is a crucial factor. But without the Resurrection faith the original community would not have come before the public to proclaim the crucified Jesus. We thus have the ingredients for a sensitive awareness of the importance of individual faith and the responsibility of that faith to be shared in the *larger* community. The believing Christian Church and the preaching Christian Church are one. The preaching function of the Church requires co-responsibility on all levels of the believing community. For "Jesus People," or any other Christians there is no possibility of being a believing Christian without the Church howsoever tarnished its institutional pediments may be.

As institutions offer more segmented and specialized activity, the individual becomes separated from the pattern of total structural norms. Individual consciousness is liberated from the social structure itself, and the freedom in the private sphere of society widens. Luckmann[74] believes that the sense of autonomy that characterizes the typical individual in modern industrialized societies is closely linked to a pervasive consumer orientation. To a higher degree than in the past, the individual is left to his own devices in choosing goods and services, friends, marriage partners, and even ultimate meanings. In brief, he is free to construct his own personal identity. Thus the modification of social structure by specialization, the emerging autonomy and pluralism related to socialization, and the "consumer" spirit prevalent in commerce and economics combine to make it more acceptable to view religion as a private affair allowing the individual to choose from an assortment of ultimate meanings in order to build his own system of ultimate meaning.

In contrast but also in connection with the individual religiosity, church religiosity may emerge as one of many manifestations of a developing institutionally non-specialized social form of religion, the difference being that it still occupies an important place among the other manifestations because of its historical connection to the traditional official Christian model. Perhaps, under the guidance of the Spirit of God, new forms will appear in connection with the traditional church allowing maximum scope to individual religiosity along with solid communal support and direction when it is needed. Because theology and developing doctrine in the pluralistic church no longer threaten the individual Christian, he might be able to internalize those valuable "traditions" of the community and thereby enter into a deep and fruitful relationship with it. The process of secularization allows autonomy and pluralism to surface and "bound off" the relevant doctrines and values of the institutional Church, leaving the whole worry of normative religion behind. In this process it is always important that the contemporary believer distinguishes his individual faith expression from that of the community. To assess this need we should recall that in the individual and social view of religion there is a cognitive base. An individual Christian sensing his gift of faith seeks to express this faith in an authentic and relevant manner. How? If the times are changing and he is confused, he looks to the community for support. In other words, he looks to a faith expression on the communal level.

A problem emerges here when we note that externalization and objectification of faith from the cognitive level generally move to the normative level. If enough people regard a certain expression of faith as appropriate, they might adopt it as a custom or norm in the community so that in turn it becomes a norm imposed on the individual believer. The individual has traditionally been comfortable with norms in the past so long as change did not occur too rapidly. However, we must admit also that the individual would not truly adopt an external social expression of religion until he internalized it, interiorized it, or saw it as valuable for his own sense of meaning of life.

Now we might add that in a rapidly changing secularized world, it is important that the individual Christian look to the theological characteristics of faith itself once again, and that he seek not to move so quickly from a cognitive to a normative expression of that faith. Perhaps it is more appropriate for the secularized man of today to reflect on the reality of the risk of faith which, based on the present understanding of God's relationship to him, reminds him of his freedom and responsibility to live out that faith in ever-changing times.

Thus, rather than stress the normative expressions of Christianity as indications of a proper world view, or adequate religiosity and faith expression for our day, the individual Christian becomes open to growth that comes from contact with several social expressions of religion related to several personal expressions of religion. Even if society tends to be normative and seeks to define principles for acting, the mature believer today is aware of his participation in an evolving experience of God within the total world community moving to the omega point or final day. A sense of the universe as evolving joined to a sensitivity of change in religious expression particularly at the cognitive level helps to alert the believer to the total adventure of a life of trust in God.

The Christian believer becomes convinced that he is moving to fuller and fuller truth in God's grace, fuller knowledge and wisdom, and the realization that these gifts centered on truth seek community for support in their expression.

Any norms acceptable in the past for a Christian expression of faith on the individual or communal level must be updated and reassessed in terms of present requirements for faith. In particular, the Christian believer's expression related to the Word of God and the Eucharist must be reassessed. Is it possible that a Christian might need to go back to a form of pre-evangelization and then gradually move forward once again examining whether his faith expressions are growing and progressing authentically and whether or not the present level of expression is truly authentic?

The secularized believer should not be threatened by changing or dwindling expressions of religion at one level when he is open to new levels of expression that could become normative if the community sees a value in determining them as such. While in the past we were wont to assess the success or failure of Christian expression, today we have a more mature sense of change, allowing for measurements to change, even blur, or become temporarily withheld, or even disappear and new expressions to be tested and, if valid, to be assimilated into the Christian life.

A sense of pluralism will allow us to envision all sorts of personal expressions of faith in religion which may or may not be used by the community supporting these individuals. Rather than seek simple norms for all people, for all times, and for all religious expression, we allow norms to be held in abeyance, or if adopted, to be open to periodic change and updating. Society as a whole has universal values related to the world view such as freedom, justice, and peace, but it devolves upon the individual Christian believer and the local community giving him support to determine how to express these values for our time.

In all humility, the individual Christian believer senses today more than ever before his limitations within his graced role as a child of God. All performance must be realistically perceived as either an authentic striving to be closer to God in a dynamic relationship of love or a lack thereof. Regardless how successful we are in empirically assessing the strength or weakness of Christianity in our milieu, we have strong support in past and present traditions to convince us of the persistence of authentic religion in the Christian community.

Summary

From the age of two onward our values reside in our keen sense of individuality that constantly demands self expression. Religion however is a rather general term. Each individual faces it in a unique manner because each has a distinct requirement to explain meaning and value for his own life. As such religion meets the needs of the individual, but provides support in a community setting.

The dominance of individuality perdures. We choose to interiorize that religion that affects our individuality most as we grow to maturity. While we normally choose the religion of our culture we choose most definitely that religion that most sharply affects our personal life.

The community is a normal support system. As such it is "expected" to support each of us as individuals. However, maturity in a psychological sense demands that we do not expect too much of society around us lest we reap disappointment and bitterness that tarnishes the optimism of personal religiousness. Perhaps it is fitting to ask: Are we comfortable with the idea that a consistent social sharing of religion is not required for every individual, and certainly not required with the consistency of the Sabbath?

By now the reader sees that I lean more toward Whitehead than toward Weber and Durkheim. I feel more stable when I anchor my sense of religion in the individual person. I stand in awe at the dignity of the individual that is not enhanced simply by being a part of a community. If anything I feel the individual tends to be lost in our present world of five billion persons. Mere numerical multiplication of individuals builds up the risk of losing the value of the individual as she or he experiences life. I continue to reflect that the collective emotions of a person in society can leave unnoticed the awesome ultimate fact which is the human being. If character depends on a person's internal conviction, we have no religion without the stability of these convictions. A person remains social by nature, but the identification of religiousness is rooted in the individual character of each person.

For Whitehead the community evolves toward individual expression of religion in which preservation of the community yields to preservation of the world. Tribal consciousness yields to world consciousness. Religion as it evolves is world-loyalty not mere local or individual loyalty. "No man is an Island' is a principle that accepts the importance of community, but hesitates to eliminate the evolution of understanding of the individual person. With Wach I see the need to combine beliefs, worship and social relationships into the full fabric of religion.

Religion as a personal phenomenon does not force me to choose between individual and communal in personal life; rather, religion tells me that each religious person transcends himself as an individual and as a member of a community in the very process of becoming a self and in establishing a world view or universal value system. The world view unites individuality with community by providing a meaning for reality when each person as person experiences reality. By joining Whitehead's idea of the individual relating to world consciousness with Luckmann's idea of the transcendence of human persons in becoming selves we see a broader picture of the healthy relationship of individual and communal in a person's life.

Review Outline

Luckmann's View of Individual and Communal Religion

World View Described by Society

Ritual - Emotion - Belief - Rationalism
(Whitehead's historical stages)

- Individual Sense of the Sacred
  (Value System + Meaning System)

- Face to Face Discussion with Friends
  (To Test Values + Meaning)

- Develop World Views and Sacred Universes

- Sacred and Profane Seen In a Relationship
  and Able to Change

Circle

of

Religion

- Religion Set Apart from Society In Age of
  Specialization and Institutionalization

- Individual Reflects on Existing World View

- Individual Today Uses Education to Combat
  Specialization

- Individual Interiorizes Personal World View As He
  Compares Personal and Societal Values

- Individual Experiences The Sacred

- Individual Shares Religious Sense

- Community (Society) and Individual In Conversation

Discussion Questions

Chapter Four

1) What is the role of desire in religion?

2) How do values relate to religion?

3) How do values and meaning relate to each other in a discussion of religion?

4) How is the desire for personal growth a religious desire?

5) How does religion fit in a world view?

6) Describe Whitehead's four historical factors in religion. Do you agree with his viewpoint?

7) What are some of the causes of secularization in our world today?

8) How does an individual relate ideally to the institutional church?

Notes

1 Gordon W. Allport, *The Individual and His Religion* (New York: The Macmillan Co., 1950), p. xi.

2 Wade Clark Roof, William McKinney, *American Mainline Religions* (New Brunswick: Rutgers University Press, 1987), p. 16.

3 Allport, *op. cit.*, pp. 4, 5.

4 *Ibid.*, p. 11.

5 *Ibid.*, p. 11.

6 *Ibid.*, p. 13.

7 *Ibid.*, p. 14.

8 *Ibid.*, p. 15.

9 *Ibid.*, p. 16.

10 *Ibid.*, p. 17.

11 Abraham Maslow, *Toward a Psychology of Being*, 2nd Edition, (New York: Van Nostrand-Reinhold, 1968), p. 206.

12 For a more detailed treatment cf. Melvin Rader and Bertram Jessup, *Art and Human Values* (Englewood Cliffs, N.J.: Prentice Hall Inc., 1973), p. 11ff.

13 G. Van der Leeuw, *Religion in Essence and Manifestation*, Vol. II (New York: Harper and Row, 1963), pp. 353, 354, 351, 352.

14 Gordon W. Allport, *op. cit.*, p. 18.

15 *Ibid.*, p. 23.

16 Thomas Luckmann, *The Invisible Religion* (New York: The Macmillan Company, 1967), p. 22.

17 *Ibid.*, p. 19.

18 Alfred North Whitehead, *Religion In the Making* (New York: New American Library, Meridian Books, 1954), p. 15.

19 *Ibid.*, p. 15.

20 *Ibid.*, p. 16.

21 Rem B. Edwards, *Reason and Religion* (New York: Harcourt, Brace, Jovanovich, Inc., 1972), p. 36 citing Durkheim, Wahl, and Yinger.

22 Alfred North Whitehead, *op. cit.*, p. 16.

23 *Ibid.*, p. 16. Akin to Whitehead's definition is that of William James in *Varieties of Religion Experience* (New York: The New American Library, Inc., Mentor Book, 1958), p. 42 in which he says religion is "the feelings, acts and experiences of individual men in their solitude, so far as they apprehend themselves to stand in relation to whatever they may consider the divine."

24 *Ibid.*, p. 19.

25 *Ibid.*, p. 20.

26 *Ibid.*, p. 21.

27 Paul W. Pruyser, *A Dynamic Psychology of Religion* (New York: Harper and Row Publishers, 1968), pp. 88-89.

28 Alfred North Whitehead, *op. cit.*, pp. 29-30.

29 *Ibid.*, p. 33.

30 *Ibid.*, p. 40.

31 *Ibid.*, p. 47

32 *Ibid.*, pp. 16, 47.

33 *Ibid.*, p. 58.

34 *Ibid.*, p. 59

35 *Ibid.*, p. 86.

36 *Ibid.*, p. 132.

37 *Ibid.*, p. 133.

38 J. Milton Yinger, "Introduction," *Religion, Society and the Individual.* J. Milton Yinger, editor (New York: The Macmillan Co., 1957), p. 12.

39 Alfred North Whitehead, *op. cit.*, p. 86.

40 J. Milton Yinger, *op. cit.*, pp. 12-17.

41 Bronislaw Malinowski, "Social and Individual Sources of Primitive Religion," *Religion, Society, and the Individual.* J. Milton Yinger, editor (New York: The Macmillan Co., 1957), p. 356.

42 *Ibid.*, pp. 357-58.

43 David Lawrence Edward, *Religion and Change* (New York: Harper and Row Publishers, 1969), p. 109.

44 *Ibid.*, p. 16.

45 *Ibid.*, p. 48.

46 Cf. Anthony F. C. Wallace, Religion, *An Anthropological View* (New York: Random House, 1966), p. 22ff.

47 Glen M. Vernon, *Sociology of Religion* (New York: McGraw-Hill Book Co., Inc., 1962), p. 94.

48 *Ibid.*, p. 94.

49 *Ibid.*, p. 105.

50 Cf. Rem B. Edwards, *op. cit.*, p. 36 footnote No. 16.

51 Thomas Luckmann, *op. cit.*, p. 22.

52 *Ibid.*, p. 36, Cf. also Philip A. Verhalen, *Faith In a Secularized World* (New York: Paulist Press, 1976).

53 *Ibid.*, p. 36.

54 *Ibid.*, p. 39.

55 *Ibid.*, p. 46.

56 *Ibid.*, p. 49.

57 *Ibid.*, p. 50.

58 *Ibid.*, p. 53.

59 *Ibid.*, p. 54, also Cf. P. Berger, *The Sacred Canopy*.

60 *Ibid.*, p. 56.

61 *Ibid.*, p. 56.

62 Robert Nisbett, *The Social Philosophers* (New York: Washington Square Press, 1973), p. 69ff.

63 *Ibid.*, p. 74.

64 *Ibid.*, p. 75.

65 Thomas Luckmann, *op. cit.*, pp. 60-61.

66 *Ibid.*, pp. 66-67.

67 *Ibid.*, p. 69.

68 *Ibid.*, p. 70.

69 *Ibid.*, pp. 75-76.

70 *Ibid.*, p. 91.

71 Kevin O'Rourke, "Are Institutions Obsolete?" Vol. 29, No. 2, *Review for Religions* (Mar. 1979), 246.

72 *Ibid.*, pp. 248-53.

73 Paulus G. Wacker, "Christus Ohne Kirche?" *Theologie Und Glaube*, 64 (1974), 1-28.

74 Thomas Luckmann, *op. cit.*, p. 98

Chapter Five

A Psychological Viewpoint

Religion behavior is difficult to measure. What seems religious for one person may not be for another. Moreover, different disciplines approach religion differently. The scientific study of religion as phenomenological is the discipline with the most basic approach. However, within this study are various aspects – historical, anthropological, philosophical, theological, sociological and psychological.

In this chapter we will attempt to look at religion from a psychological view point. As inquirers we must accept the adventure of new terms and expressions. However, psychology's particular interest in the human person will help us look at religion in a less "churchy," less denominational, less cultural manner. Ideally, this particular dimension of religion will shed light on our total study of the subject.

Historical Considerations

We Americans are accustomed to consider William James as the father of the psychology of religion on the basis of *The Varieties of Religious Experience*.[1] When psychologists turn their attention to the religious behavior of individuals they feel confident that religious activities of men and women are worth trying to understand, and furthermore with James' encouragement are capable of being understood. The ways open to science for this investigation are three:

method-centered,
system-centered, and
problem-centered.

If we use a special method or a theoretical system we often attempt to fit observations into pre-conceived molds. Only the problem-centered approach deters us from building bias toward conclusions. When we ask: "What is this scientific activity called the psychology of religion?" we confront the variety of experiences that touch us in our daily life. Orlo Strunk says:

> So let us define the psychology of religion as that branch of general psychology which attempts to understand, control, and predict human behavior — both propriate and peripheral — which is perceived as being religious by the individual, and which is susceptible to one or more of the methods of psychological science.[2]

Obviously, there are many definitions of the psychology of religion, but this choice covers the subject area sufficiently for our general study. As Strunk stresses, the primary function of the psychology of religion is understanding.

Religious Behavior

Religious behavior, like all behavior, means more than motor responses. It includes such things as beliefs and verbalized thoughts and values. This behavior may be either propriate or peripheral. Propriate behavior refers to the kind of behavior perceived as being personal, warm, and immensely important by the individual, as compared to peripheral behavior, which is impersonal, cold and relatively unimportant. Both types of behavior are legitimate areas of study for the psychology of religion.

In religious activity it is necessary that the behavior be perceived as religious by the individual. This narrows our field of interest from the general to the psychological. Religion can be understood in many ways, but we are primarily interested in how the human person sees his behavior as religious.

Psychological Organization of Religion

Strunk views religion as an organization of cognitive – affective – conative factors perceived by the individual as being religious in nature, and of being especially appropriate or inappropriate in achieving self-adequacy.[3] Again, from a psychological standpoint, we say, religion is only religion when the perceiver perceives it as such. To enter into greater depth, Strunk treats each of the factors –

cognitive - or - Beliefs
affective - or - Feelings,
conative - or - Actions

– separately. This division is convenient but not necessary, and certainly not the only practical division of the material available.

At the turn of the 20th century, E. S. Ames wrote a psychology of religion with a strong functional orientation. Later Trout (1931) used a behavioristic stress. In 1958, W. H. Clark produced a study heavy with personalistic psychology. More recently Paul E. Johnson (1959) used a more interpersonal orientation. However, for the sake of an orderly examination of the material we will utilize Strunk's division. At this point we turn to Strunk's postulates[4] basic to the study:

1) All behavior, without exception, is completely determined by and pertinent to, the perceptual field of the behaving organism. By the perceptual field is meant the entire universe including one's self, as it is experienced by the individual at the instant of action. In our study of the psychology of religion we look to that area defined as religious by the behaving organism.

2) Secondly, the basic need of human beings is to achieve self-adequacy. Basically, all of a person's behavior is seen as an attempt to maintain his phenomenal self and to make it more adequate. This phenomenal self (perceived self) is not merely the physical self, but the self as perceived. Note that perception of one's self is the central issue in the study of religion and religious behavior.

The adequate person, perceptually speaking, is one who has achieved a high degree of need satisfaction. Generally, such people are quite successful in coping with life and in maintaining and enhancing life.

3) Thirdly, a person is a self-actualizing creature. Since behavior is determined by and pertinent to perception, individuals must be free to act in reference to their perceptions. Thus each has the capacity for self-actualization. Behavior in this case is the result not only of external conditions but also of internal processes such as ideas, attitudes and needs.

In these three basic postulates the self is the center of discussion. In general, we can call "self" the knower, or subject, or passive organizer and rationalizer. We understand this idea of self in the context of Strunk's *modified field theory*.[5]

"Field" in physics refers to all the forces surrounding an object and which in turn helps to determine the various properties of the object. An example often provided is that of a rolling ball. The "behavior" of the ball is determined by both properties inherent in the ball and field forces acting upon it. This concept of "field" is helpful in attempting to understand human behavior. Field theory in psychology maintains that each individual exists in an environmental field that is constantly changing. In order to predict one individual's behavior Strunk contends that it is necessary to comprehend both his field and the inner properties of the person. Because the perceptual field determines behavior (postulate #1) and this perceptual field is the entire universe, we must try to discover what an individual perceives. It may not be in accord with an observer's perceptions, but his individual perception alone determines behavior.

The Phenomenal Self

The phenomenal self (or perceptual self) is the portion of the total field (phenomenal field) which the individual regards as part of a characteristic of himself. The unique way each of us sees ourself makes up the phenomenal self. I may see myself as a great athlete, but from a more objective viewpoint I may be mediocre. Regardless, the pattern (or Gestalt) of all these perceptions is the phenomenal self or "I" who seeks out a way of perceiving all reality.

Just as the phenomenal self is part of the perceptual field the self-concept is part of the phenomenal self. The self-concept represents an organization of perceptions which seem especially important to the individual.[6] He or she cannot conceive of himself without these aspects. Thus, three concepts – the phenomenal field, the phenomenal self, and the self-concept – are basic to our study of religion.

Religion and the Self System

All perceptions ever made, both clear and vague, go into the construction of the self. Our attention centers on the religious factors of experiences perceived. When the religious factor is easily identified, such as in praying, there is no problem. The self clearly knows he or she is acting religiously. However, many other factors in our perceived experiences are less obvious. In these cases we must accept the judgment of the "behaver" or experiencer. If a person says his behavior is religious, it is religious.

The Beginnings of the Self System

As the infant grows he or she gradually distinguishes the self from the rest of its environment. Because all religion must be learned (differentiated) it takes years before one could be considered religious. When a child is cast out into the world of stimuli, the raw materials for the development of the self system begin to make their marks. At first the infant's perceptions are fuzzy. Gradually differentiation of stimuli and experiences takes place. Eventually behavior becomes specific. From these first perceptual events comes the discovery of the self. Soon the child can distinguish between the "me" and "not me."

Unfortunately, up to now we know little about the specific ways in which children learn to perceive themselves. Likewise, we know little of how children first perceive religious objects. In the factors of the phenomenal self, religious factors do not present themselves until quite late in childhood. Yet Sophia Pahs[7] contends that we begin to create our religion, our philosophy of life immediately from the time of birth. Important in this development are the feelings and values of adults around us.

What the psychologists agree upon is that later religious perceptions are determined by previous experiences of a non-religious nature. At an early age the child cannot differentiate religious and non-religious perceptions. Yet, all kinds of experiences leave their mark on a child which will color later perceptions of a religious nature. In the Boys Town Study,[8] the researchers found that a child who had a congenial home life generally had a good feeling toward God, and tended to be religious. Of various studies (Jones, Freud, Stevenson, Nelson and James, Strunk) relating parent images with the image of God, regardless of the maternal, or paternal stress, there seemed to be some correlation between a healthy view of parents and that of God.

We go back to the principle: those things which satisfy our need for self-adequacy are valued. In the early stages of development those objects which satisfy this need are rarely perceived as religious, yet the way in which self-adequacy is obtained in the early stages sets the trend for later perceptions of a kind called religious by a perceiver.

Need

Strunk defines need as "the lack of something which, if present, would tend to further the welfare of the organism or of the species, or to facilitate its usual behavior."[9] Henry A. Murray (1938) and Abraham Maslow (1954) have done extensive study on the hierarchy of needs. However need theories are complex and agreement about basic needs is often difficult to determine. Needs may range from one to one hundred. Maslow lists five basic needs.[10] In hope of avoiding a dispute Arthur Combs and Donald Snygg claim there is but one basic need, the need for self-adequacy. Religious behavior, according to Strunk is one significant way of achieving self-adequacy.

Cognitive Aspects of Religion

Needs and perceptions are psychological indicators telling us much about religious behavior. But we should also study beliefs and attitudes as phenomena of a higher order in our study of religion. We are not interested presently in the theology of belief. Rather we look to the psychological study of belief, that is, how a person acts in accordance with his beliefs. A belief is considered psychologically true if such a belief is held by some persons.

Interested in the cognitive and perceptual aspects of the term we try to describe what belief is. David Krech and Richard Crutchfield claim: "A belief is an enduring organization of perceptions and cognitions about some aspect of the individual's world."[11]

Beliefs are verifiable; whereas faith refers to matters intrinsically unverifiable such as the existence and nature of God. Beliefs are less complex than faith. Faith moreover, is highly propriate in nature, i.e., it is warm and close to the individual. This is not necessarily true of beliefs. In real life there is little distinction between religious beliefs and religious faith. In fact, religious beliefs are clung to and are deeply regarded with the same tenacity as religious faith. One reason is that religious beliefs tend to be unverifiable and consequently fall into the category of faith as a very personal or propriate experience.

Beliefs and Needs

The statement that needs determine beliefs is true enough to command our respect. An individual, for example, may have a strong need for safety and may partially meet this need by believing he is one of God's children under His direct care and protection. The basic need however is to maintain and enhance the perceived self. Ordinarily there are plenty of beliefs available to handle the average person's life situation. Most people take ready made beliefs in society and internalize them to meet their specific needs.

Sociology in contrast to psychology would call these beliefs "value systems." Most often we internalize the value systems of society around us. As such they are religious and tend to meet our needs.

As we grow older we discard simple, authoritarian beliefs for more complex and personal beliefs. Beliefs develop and change to meet the new needs of the individual's immediate situation. In a person's constant attempt to create or enhance an adequate self, new beliefs must be internalized. To fail to do this leads to arrested growth. The pathology of religion reveals that religious persons who doggedly retain childish beliefs in the face of highly complex situations often slide into bigotry and other states considered "abnormal" by society.

If we accept one basic need the need for self-adequacy, we can move forward in our attempt to discover the various ways religious factors, such as beliefs may be related to the maintenance and enhancement of the perceived self. The primary function of religious beliefs from a psychological viewpoint is to achieve self-adequacy. We believe only what in one way or another maintains or enhances our perceived self. But let us not rest with this simple statement. The precise ways in which religious beliefs fulfill this function are complex and little known. We must admit the lack of empirical information about this problem.

While there is a correlation between biological needs and religious practices, the questions of psychology run deeper than this record of history of religious practices. Man as a sound animal acts from highly complex motives. What we are basically asking is how does a person internalize his beliefs so that they show his desire to achieve self-adequacy?

Beginning with the principle that a person behaves in ways consistent with his beliefs we enter into complexities that nullify the principle. For example, a person may lament: "All my life I believed I should love my enemies, but I didn't." The answer to this problem is the verifiable indication that religion may manifest itself on a meaning line from little or no intensity to great intensity. Religion in one is acute fever, in another a dull habit and in a third, a mere convention accepted by society. For one a self concept needs strong involvement in religious beliefs and for another only slight involvement is necessary. Yet both persons may have a good sense of self-adequacy supported in different ways by his or her religious beliefs. What distinguishes propriate religious beliefs from periph-eral beliefs is that propriate beliefs are deeply internalized often going to the very core of the self-concept.

Beliefs and Culture

Most of our religious beliefs are greatly influenced by our cul-ture. The fact that most Americans are Christians and not Muslims attests to this observation. Yet how a culture precisely influences our personal religious beliefs is difficult to determine.

L. Festinger[12] maintains that beliefs, opinions, and cognitive at-titudes need to be evaluated by the individual person. As each per-son evaluates beliefs, she or he compares them with other people's beliefs. Religious beliefs and convictions are not easily amenable to scientific or empirical verification. In order to maintain such be-liefs the individual must compare his beliefs with those of other people. In other words, social support is necessary to maintain be-liefs that are impossible to prove. Festinger believes that the eval-uative process is possible only when the opinions of the social group are fairly close to those expressed by the person concerned. Such a person is likely to be attracted to that group of persons who hold similar opinions and beliefs, and will derive social support for her beliefs by belonging to the group. L. B. Brown provided similar support for a cognitive system (1962) separate from personality factors that requires strong social support for its maintenance.

In one study Strunk shows that some cultures show a greater need for religion than other cultures. Some cultures such as Israel, find ways other than religious to maintain and enhance their phe-nomenal self. While certain doctrines or beliefs are believed less and less (virgin birth, a literal heaven and hell) certain abstract reli-gious beliefs (dignity of man, eternal governing principle) are held over the years with a relatively great degree of stability.

For some of us weight watchers, we are what we eat; for the lit-erate, we are what we read; and for psychologists and sociologists we are what we experience. Besides eating, reading and experi-encing we have a whole culture surrounding us and promoting in stimulating and sly ways a manner of living that may or may not relate to our beliefs and values. If all this is true, how do we explain our religious behavior? Professor Allport[12] tells the story of the young undergraduate who, after hearing Archbishop William Temple give an address at Oxford opened up the discussion by commenting, "Well, of course, Archbishop, the point is that you believe what you believe because of the way you were brought up." To which, so the story goes, the Archbishop quietly and coolly replied, "That is as it may be. But the fact remains that you believe that I believe what I believe because of the way I was brought up, because of the way you were brought up." The Archbishop simply and politely pointed out that such a statement of belief and cultural influence is nothing more than an entry into an infinite logical regress. The atomic unity of all history and of all persons' experiences is an interesting basis for development of ideas, but the individual and her choice of beliefs cannot be lost in such a cosmic view.

We repeat that religious beliefs do determine behavior, yet in a given community holding common religious beliefs there is often a wide range of behavior. What this issue proves is that the relationship between religion and behavior is not easily determined.[14]

Thus, from a psychological standpoint we are interested how a person interacts with religion. If a person acts from needs and his behavior shows a quest for self-adequacy, his religious life will somehow fit into this pattern. Beliefs function as aids to man's need for adequacy. But, because the self-system evolves and changes, beliefs too will change to correspond to the total picture of self-organization. The problem remains: in this common system called human living how do beliefs affect behavior?

Affective Aspects of Religion

Early psychologists of religion concentrated on the religious experience as perhaps the most engaging aspect of the study. Particularly did the conversion experience capture the scientist's attention since it was considered so humanly dramatic. But most important, because psychology must start from experience, the psychological study of religion must start from what people consider their religious experience.

Religious Experience as Perception

Every experience has an emotional dimension to it. Because religion is concerned with the deepest needs and the highest values of life, it will naturally be charged with emotional urgency. Although emotions are described variously depending on the experience, the bodily processes that occur under the emotion are the same. "Emotion," according to Strunk, is a "kind of acceleration of certain bodily processes."[15] In some cases, such as peyotism, body processes account for a large portion of the religious experience. Whatever the level of emotion it must be regarded as one distinct aspect of an organism's search for self-adequacy. Whenever the organism perceives itself to be in a situation which threatens the self, emotional reactions take place.

The closer the perceived experience comes to the self-concept, the greater degree of emotional experience. When the experience is more propriate than peripheral, the emotional reaction is stronger. For example, a picture of the Virgin Mary perceived by an individual may or may not elicit an emotional response. To a devout Mediterranean Roman Catholic this may be a propriate relationship to the phenomenal self and consequently the emotional response will be great. On the other hand, the same picture may elicit little or no response from an American Protestant.

Feeling vs. Emotions

Whereas emotion is an acceleration of certain bodily processes, feelings are descriptions of our perceptual fields at a particular moment.[16] Based on the complexity of our perceptual field, we frequently find it difficult to describe our feelings. Mystics past and present tell of the great difficulty describing their feelings during a religious experience.

In a religious experience in which we are drawn to God, the time of the event coincides with our self-concept developing a sense of adequacy in relation to the universe and to the supreme orderer of the universe. So, for a particular ministerial student who felt he was a Christian leader without a religious experience, there was a need to achieve greater self-adequacy. Within a short time he had a religious experience that he considered decisive to his vocation. Moreover this religious experience drew several religious factors into a meaningful pattern of self-perceptions. These various religious factors – church, scripture, conversion – now were internalized. They penetrated to the core of his self-concept A definite religious sense of unification of life ensued.

Once again we state, the perception of environmental factors and bodily processes determine the individual's behavior.[17] Thus any religious experience would take a variety of forms depending on these two characteristics of behavior. In his *Varieties of Religious Experience* William James alerts us to the possibility of several types of religious experience. However, he classifies these experiences into two main types:

the "once born" and
the "twice born".

Stated another way, there is the "gradual" religious experience (or conversion experience) and the "sudden" religious experience (conversion experience). Actually there are no two religious experiences exactly alike. In each case a unique set of self perceptions comes in contact with a unique set of situational factors.

Nevertheless, religious experiences have enough in common for us to speak of various forms of religious experience. The individual who grows into a religious person without any conspicuous and traumatic events gives the impression that a simple but steady process is at work. In actuality, the process is quite complex. This "gradual" or "once born" experience shows a consistent and rather smooth internalization of religious factors. Throughout most of his life this person has found religious factors quite satisfactory in his search for self-adequacy. On the surface there is little conflict involved in the internalization process.

Under closer examination, it is found that these persons often experience internalization pains. There are times when religious factors conflict with one another and with non-religious factors.

One example would be the gradual and persistent growth of a committed Christian closely tied to a warm and loving Christian community. During this development there are times of decision, of conflict, of puzzlement but always the person is striving for self-adequacy. He hesitates, experiments, makes mistaken judgments, but his self perceptions are tied to a total commitment to religious factors. Thus the development was gradual, at times slow, with crooks, and turns and bends in the road, but never did he move in a completely opposite direction. Such is the "once born" person.

"Twice Born"

It is the "twice born" person who has received the most attention in psychological and popular literature. The sudden, dramatic, "about face" conversion is obviously more exciting. Psychologically speaking, the process involved in a sudden religious experience is the same as the gradual form of religious experience. Thus, religious factors move from the periphery of the self-system to the core, the self-concept itself. The unique aspect is that this movement appears to occur suddenly.

Take for example the story of Paul, or John Wesley, or a neighbor friend who suddenly felt that God was directing him to change his life, become religious and committed to some expression of this religious conversion. The "twice born" person speaks of a sudden change in his perceptual field.

The person who has this type of experience normally is not consciously aware of any great deliberation upon religious or theological topics, nor is there any conflict over religious issues. Then, quite suddenly something dramatic and startling occurs that changes the whole tenor of his life. This transformation of attitudes and beliefs often produces a distinct behavioral change. The occasion of change may vary from a sudden experience filled with emotion to one calling for a dramatic decision. Some psychologists[18] explain this sudden conversion as an experience of conflict and frustration repressed into the unconscious. One day a relief from unconscious tension causes a dramatic reversal of beliefs and attitudes resulting in a refreshing emotional release of joy and elation.

For some theologians the repression of conflict and frustration seems an inadequate explanation when one is required to explain more extreme experiences recorded at some of the meetings addressed by evangelists like John Wesley. The screaming, swooning, fainting and convulsions of every description seem to be an excessive response to repressed conflict and frustration. A mere physiological explanation tied to psychological theories is not a complete explanation for the unique character of an individual's sudden conversion, but these studies of conversions over the years shed some dim light on the many solid possible reasons for sudden dramatic conversions that many individuals experience.

Scobie adds a third conversion experience called an unconscious conversion. In a typical example of unconscious conversion, a child brought up in a Jewish or Christian home gradually comes to accept the beliefs of his parents. There is almost no indication of theological or moral conflict in the child's life. In this group religion is merely a social condition with no "commitment" strings attached. Throughout their growth process these persons' belief in God remains undisturbed and unchallenged.

Conversion in the Acts of the Apostles

Lest we think that there is actually only one type of genuine conversion experience, *The Acts of the Apostles* reports how different kinds of people with vastly different backgrounds are brought to faith in Christ through a variety of circumstances. In the end, all claim to share the same faith convictions. Let us consider only a few examples in the Acts. In chapter eight there is an account of the conversion of an Ethiopian leader. He is described as a responsible man making a pilgrimage to Jerusalem. Along the way he reads the Scriptures (verses 27, 28). With Philip's aid he seeks more knowledge from the Scriptures to add to his considerable previous knowledge about God. Eager to learn about Christianity, he shows a remarkable willingness to make a decision to become a Christian once the issues become clear.

The next chapter of Acts, chapter nine, gives the well known account of the conversion of Saul of Tarsus, a man with a detailed knowledge of Judaism and the Jewish Scriptures, and likewise with an equally detailed knowledge of the beliefs of the early Christians, considering his recent occupation had been the persecution of the Christians (verses one and two). We might speculate that since witnessing the martyrdom of Stephen (Acts 7/58) Paul may well have had a growing conviction of the truth of the beliefs of these Christians as he pondered the amazing way in which Stephen died. In verse three Saul is subjected to a traumatic experience on the road to Damascus. From both a psychological and theological point of view volumes have been written on this experience. Most scholars agree that the result was clear. There was a struggle and then a decision expressed in his question: "Who are you, Lord?" and the response: "I am Jesus and you are persecuting me," (verse five).

In chapter ten we read of a man who would today be described as a Company Commander in the armed services (verse one). From the succeeding verses it becomes clear that he is a religious man and that he and his whole family joined in the worship of God. With an attitude of expectancy and an experience of a vision from God he seeks further instruction from the apostle Peter, and moves to a decision. (verse 25 and 33). In chapter sixteen we have an account of a woman whom we are told is already a worshipper of God (verse 14). The narrative tells how she sits and talks to her friends and more or less puts the gospel into her ongoing conversation. Paul joined this little group and shared their leisurely discussion. Just how often this occurred before the woman became a Christian we do not know, but it seems clear that once she had become acquainted with the truth of the Christian message, she became a Christian (verse 15).

These episodes in Acts illustrate the range of experiences and backgrounds that provided one common outcome: belief in God and Christ whom he sent. To focus on the psychological aspects of these conversions does not mean that one ignores or denies that it is the truth that grips the mind of the hearer rather than the stirring of the emotions that is the prime ingredient in any conversion experience. What the Bible makes eminently clear is that, for all the diversity of background and circumstances of these conversions, they took place because God acted. For example in the case of the Ethiopian leader, we are told that it was the Lord who directed Philip to go to the Gaza road (Acts 8:26), and it was the Spirit who told Philip to "Go and meet that chariot" (8:29). In the case of Saul it was the Lord who directed him to "Get up now and go into the city" (9:6). It was the Lord who gave Ananias his instructions (9:15) to go and help Saul. The centurian was directed by an angel of God to send for Peter (10:3), and The Holy Spirit "came down on all the listeners" (10:44). Of the woman Lydia we are told it was the Lord who opened her heart to accept what Paul was saying (16:14). The point is clear and profound.

In the Acts of the Apostles as in other books of the New Testament we learn that a person turns to God and the gospel only because God has first begun to work in him.

Whether we study conversion from the standpoint of the psychologist or from the accounts given in the Bible, it is clear that a conversion is at once a profound experience and an extremely complex process. Malcolm Jeeves reminds us of the range of different predisposing factors and accompanying behavioral changes involved in a conversion.[19] Moreover, we must remember that conversion is not something that is exclusive to the Christian faith, but that there are conversions to other kinds of religious and to various non-religious systems of belief, such as political ones. In the next section we shall describe how both the "once born" and the "twice born" experience the same process, i.e., a unique set of self-perceptions coming in contact with a unique set of situational factors. The interrelationship resulting is a unique perceptual field − a field difficult to describe, but one which, nevertheless, determines behavior.[20]

Describing Religious Feelings

Feelings call for the verbalizations of our perceptual field at a particular moment. Feelings are the result of an interrelationship of self perceptions and perceptions of a situation. What makes feelings religious are the perceivers' interpretation. In each case depending on his vocabulary or ability to articulate his experience, depending on the context of his life and the purpose for the description there will be variation in describing the religious experience. The three factors involved are:

A) Vocabulary: We must be cautious lest literate sophistication becomes a measure of the depth of the religious experience.

B) Greater Content: Culture will be a significant factor in any description of a religious experience. A person raised in a Christian environment would not express his religious experience in Buddhist terminology. Sociologists spend a great amount of time studying the implications of this factor.

C) Intention of the Reporter: The motive or intentions of the reporter will affect the description of the religious experience. Naturally, each of us looks to honesty for the foundation of any valuable description.

The description of religious feelings is important because these feelings lead to changes in behavior. Thus changes in behavior are the direct result of changes in the perceptual field. The more radical the change in the perceptual field, the more conspicuous will be the changes in behavior.

Religious perceptions result in religious behavior. Obviously, at times, the observable behavior may not be apparently religious. This occurs when the observer's field is not similar to that of the behaver. If the religious factors in the psychological field are strong and deep, the person is saturated with religious propensity. Much or most of his behavior will be religious.

Because any experience can have religious significance for an individual, systematic analysis of personal experiences is extremely difficult. What is more important is not so much the kind of experience, but the way various experiences cohere and relate to one another to produce some sort of religious effect such as commitment.[21]

The Movement Toward Conversion

Conversion research indicates that keen religious interest peaks around the age of fifteen or sixteen. At the same time, according to general information, a decline in church attendance and an increase in doubt about religious matters occurs. Argyle[22] suggests that this is an age when many decisions are made including the one for or against religious commitment. Because only a relatively small number choose to become "religious," the conversion phenomenon is concealed by the general decline in religious activity by the majority of adolescents. "In general," according to Scobie, "a conversion is more likely to be permanent if it is gradual."[23] In gradual conversion the adoption of beliefs is much slower and therefore likely to be more thorough whereas the sudden converts background of religious thought and consideration is somewhat limited. In some cases the "twice born" or sudden convert may know little more than what he has just learned from the evangelist leading him to conversion.

Based on a variety of research data about believers in our typical Judeo-Christian atmosphere of America, Scobie charts the religious development of three conversion types: the once born or gradual conversion, the twice born or sudden conversion and the unconscious conversion. As a child passes through the normal stages of cognitive development, he develops concomitantly his religious thinking. Goldman[24] links religious development closely to the three stages of thinking developed by Piaget: intuitive, concrete, and eventually, abstract thinking. The child passes through each stage and by the time he reaches adolescence, his religious thinking has normally reached the abstract stage. It is at this stage that the individual adolescent begins to challenge the beliefs derived from his home or church atmosphere. This too is the stage when the various conversion processes begin to develop.

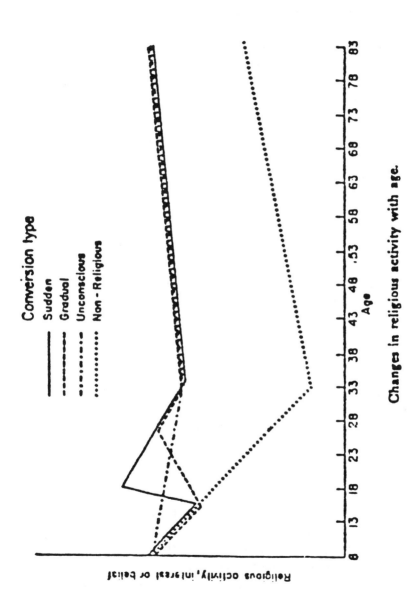

Changes in religious activity with age.

Courtesy of Goeffrey F. W. Scobie.

In the unconscious conversion group the process continues with passive or somewhat positive acceptance. For the sudden or gradual convert the process is interrupted experience. As the chart shows, for a majority of people, the conversion process continues in a negative direction from the onset of puberty. Depending on the conversion type, the individual person will return to the "fold" usually after the age of 30. This development system described by Scobie is dependent on our typical Western culture. In cultures other than ours, there may be a different developmental pattern. Notice that for the unconscious conversion group the decline or redirection is very gradual throughout the life of the believer. Also, we must further note that while this chart portrays a sharp distinction among the three groups, it does not strive for statistical accuracy.

The charting by Scobie is based on religious activities, interest or belief. He notes that most of the information provided for the study treats of religious activities (behavior) and not religious belief or interest. Overall, the chart shows that there is a gradual increase in religious activity and belief as a person moves beyond the age of thirty. This increase seems to be more a function of age and maturity than of historical events or environment. The whole panoply of attitudes and reflections that develop with approaching middle age impacts on the life of the believer in our particular culture. While conversion experiences occur in most religions, they do not appear to have the same importance as they do in Christianity. Perhaps future research will cast some light on this trait of Christianity.

Summary

Religious experience is central to the studying of the psychology of religion. Emotions are present, but more important are the feelings connected with a religious experience, i.e., the descriptions of our perceptual fields at a particular moment.

Whether the religious experience is "gradual" or "sudden," the psychological process is the same. In both forms self-perceptions come in contact with a situation. In the "gradual" experience the process is relatively mild and inconspicuous. In the case of sudden conversion the influx of situational factors of a religious sort take place in a short period of time. Both forms create perceptual fields which determine behavior. Again we note the relationship between religious feelings and behavior is direct.

Conative Aspects of Religion

In the context of our phenomenological orientation we reflect on key behavioral events in religion. The behavioral events discussed here are: prayer, worship, ritual and nonreligious acts. We must stress that perception remains superior to the observable behavior. Recalling that the basic need in human beings is to maintain and enhance the perceived self, we will begin our discussion of the first of these typical religious behavioral acts.

Prayer

Prayer is a typically clear-cut example of religious behavior. Both behaver and observer perceive this activity as religious. For the psychologist of religion prayer is one event that is readily open to study.

Why do individuals pray? Recent studies show that every typical Westerner prays at some time in his or her life. What is the motivation factor? A. T. Welford in a study using anecdotes or stimulus material sought to discover if prayer is dependent upon frustration or affliction. His conclusions were that any simple hypothesis which regards prayer as a response merely to distressing, threatening forces is inadequate. Moreover, neither frustration nor affliction *alone* is adequate to account for prayer; yet together they appear to account for a large part of the co-variation in this experiment.[25]

These findings move beyond Freud's theory that religious behavior is a response to a particular environment which prevents adjustment in a normal manner. Because prayer represents one form of behavior we must say that it is a way that the individual has found useful in achieving self-adequacy − in maintaining and enhancing the perceived self. Prayer, therefore is not utilized merely in time of stress, but also when the individual finds himself secure and sound.

But how does prayer lead to self-adequacy? Strunk[26] points out two ways:

1) Prayer as a reflective process, gives an individual a chance to *evaluate* himself in a *relatively secure* context. During the day we constantly define our relationships to people and events within our perceived self, but prayer offers the unique opportunity for self evaluation since it tends to eliminate the social stimuli that might color the evaluation. Prayers of petition, thanksgiving and reparation clarify the self-concept sharply, thus lending to precise behavior. This is especially true of disciplined prayer whereby the individual makes prayer an important part of his everyday life. Prayer simply felt as "talking to oneself" has psychological benefits because it is an excellent context for reflection and evaluation.

2) Prayer provides an *opportunity* for *extended identification*. The ability for identification is undoubtedly formed early in the socialization process. In the early years of life the organism is self-centered to an extreme degree, but in the developmental process the child learns to invest himself in external objects. Beginning with the family the child slowly expands his or her horizons to include church, state, and so on. If this extension of the self is successful – i.e., if it leads to the maintenance and enhancement of the perceived self – it will become a regular and valued way of dealing with the world.

"In prayer," Strunk says, "the opportunity for identification is greatest in that the object of prayer is perceived as being the most comprehensive and value-laden of all objects, God himself."[27]

Thus prayer is but a particular form of religious behavior having jas a psychological goal self-adequacy. Yet, while we have stressed what the external observer might like to call "mature" or disciplined prayer, the propriate nature of the prayer act like all religious acts is dependent on the prayer's world.

Worship

All actions, including religious actions, require energy, power and authority. In Western religions, the creator is the fountainhead who gives consent for their application. The divine power moves to the believer, and based on his benevolence, bestows his energy, power and authority on the leaders of the people as well as the people themselves. The occasions are feast days and special times of worship; the persons receiving the divine power are usually shamans, elders and priests.

In this manner a portion of all human activities are set aside as religious activities or work to be done for the "gods." Worship is work. It is the active side of religion. For the Buddhist, worship is a kind of giving; for the Hebrew and later on for the modern Jews, it is service. The Greek word liturgy means "work of the people."[28] The Germans speak of Gottesdienst, i.e. service to God. The Latin term *cult* means caring, maintaining, exercising, honoring and serving. One reason for the work of worship is imitation. A human person does on a small scale what the deity does on a large scale. Modern Christians - Catholics and Protestants - celebrate a symbolic common meal. It is a memorial to Christ's Last Supper, who in turn was celebrating a much older memorial meal, the Passover, which symbolized the liberation of Israel from Egyptian slavery through a special act of God. The imitation slips gradually into identification. As we enact the worship ceremony we begin to identify with the event and with the principal celebrant of the event, Jesus Christ, the modern high priest.

Much of what we said about prayer pertains to worship. This event likewise occurs to satisfy the need for self-adequacy. Strunk believes that worshipful acts are attempts to codify self-perceptions. The worshiper's perception of the nature of God makes a difference in the perceptual field and therefore in behavior. Likewise if the individual perceives himself to be a good public worshiper and a faithful church-goer, he will worship, even though he may not accept the implicit requirements of worship. Indeed he may be an agnostic; yet, public worship activity is needed by him and he will continue to worship as long as it satisfies his search for self-adequacy. Another person, because he affirms God when he accepts Him in a I-Thou context has a propriate feeling for worship. Hence, worship is crucial in his achievement of self-adequacy. A third person may worship in order to impress his potential clients or to sell insurance or used cars. Worship to him also is propriate but for different reasons not linked to a faith in a personal God.

Ritual

Ritual is a prescribed form of activity determined by considerations of tradition and symbolism. Ritual takes place in the context of worship, and it is modified according to the needs of the time. When it is prescribed it has proved itself. If it ceases to work it is changed or discarded. "Rituals are codified behavioral acts," remarks Strunk, "which have satisfied the individual's search for self-adequacy over a long period of time."[29]

People with a strong need for patterned living are drawn to ritualistic religion. Thus while a person may be very religious, his need for ritual will depend on other psychological needs. Again Strunk reminds us that all acts are performed to achieve self-adequacy.

Non-Religious Acts

The problem perdures: how does one relate religiousness to various behavioral acts? The difficulty is that for an individual person propriate and peripheral factors in a given act must be weighed.

Moreover, all behavior is completely determined by the perceptual field of the behaving organism. Basically it is difficult for an outside observer to say that a perceiver perceives an act as religious or non-religious. If the perceptual field is saturated with religious factors, then most of the behavior will be perceived as religious by the behaver. Some people with a wide range of religious beliefs interpret all of life as a religious drama. For such persons there is no such thing as non-religious behavior. For example, consider the attitude of a religious brother working in a kitchen. For him washing pots and pans can be a basically religious activity bringing him into intimate contact with his God. The perceiver, not the observer is meant to estimate if a certain act is religious or non-religious. The observer must rely on the perceiver's report of his perceptual field.

Integration of Cognitive, Affective and Conative Aspects

The human person is a problem-confronting, problem-solving creature. From the moment of birth he or she is faced with a host of difficult situations or problems. The heart of every problem is how to achieve self-adequacy. In order to solve this key problem the individual makes use of many factors, some of which are religious. For example, prayer, belief systems, ritual are all religious factors able to assist some people to face the various problems of life. If these religious factors help the person they are internalized so that for all practical purposes they become part of the person. Once internalized these religious factors serve the person as long as they help solve the great problem of life – e.g., sickness, accident, tragedy, death, and alienation.

Religious factors frequently serve individuals better than other systems or factors because they give more adequate answers to the great problems of life asked by all of us. "What's it all about, Alfie?" "Is that all there is?" are modern day lyrical witnesses to the perennial questions affecting the human species. Self adequacy requires a certain, if limited, understanding of the meaning of life. Religion, better than science, commerce, art or politics, is able to give some answers to these questions of life's meaning. Even a person who has mental illness can gain help from religious factors in finding meaning for his perceptual field.

Some people may not "seem" to use religious factors to put meaning in their life. However, it is difficult to estimate the role of religion in a person's life beyond the impressions that strike the perceiver (behaver) – himself. This difficulty should make us aware of the limitations of the psychology of religion. Psychology can take note only of the human psychical side. The nature and activity of God, (or the "ultimate concern") cannot become the object of scientific inquiry. Philosophical and theological questions related to religion occupy these areas, and the psychology or religion must avoid confusing its role with that of philosophy and theology.

When we say human being, and human activity we must admit to a person capable of experiencing philosophical and theological factors within his religious factors. Thus the human person has a philosophy of God, and a theology of God along with religious factors and activities all tied together showing him that he has religious attitudes in his perceptual field.

We want to understand religion in its widest possible context. The psychology of religion in its limited goals tells us about the activity of the individual person who perceives he is religious. As a discipline psychology tells us how this person views reality with or without these religious factors.

The psychology of religion looks more to the individual than to the community, but we assume this accent on the individual because of the nature of the investigation. By contrast in the next chapter we will turn to the object of religion in Western society - God. We will view God in a most up-to-date fashion but this study will be more of a communal and cerebral investigation that leaves individual and psychological concerns aside.

Discussion Questions

Chapter Five

1) Distinguish and describe the cognitive, affective and conative elements of religious behavior.

2) Discuss the value of understanding a "modified" field theory for personal living.

3) Distinguish the three types of conversion experiences.

Notes

1 Orlo Strunk, Jr., *Religion A Psychological Interpretation* (New York: Abingdon Press, 1962), p. 17.

2 *Ibid.*, p. 20.

3 *Ibid.*, p. 22.

4 *Ibid.*, p. 25.

5 *Ibid.*, p. 26.

6 *Ibid.*, p. 28.

7 *Ibid.*, p. 33.

8 Hart M. Nelson, Raymond H. Potvin, and Joseph Shields, *The Religion of Children* (Washington D.C.: United States Catholic Conference, 1977).

9 Orlo Strunk, Jr., *op. cit.*, p. 40.

10 The basic needs according to Maslow are found in five groupings: 1) Physiological needs, i.e. the need for food, drink and rest to maintain bodily health. 2) Safety needs, i.e. security, stability, protection, freedom from anxiety, need for order. 3) Belongingness and love needs, i.e. need for roots, for family contact and love. 4) Esteem needs, i.e., the need for a firmly based usually high evaluation of self. This need grouping involves a desire for achievement, independence and freedom. 5) Self actualization, i.e. the need to be true to one's nature and achieve a full expression of self. Cf. Abraham H. Maslow, *Motivation and Personality* (New York: Harper and Row Publishers, 1970), pp. 35ff.

11 *Ibid.*, p. 42.

12 Geoffrey E. W. Scobie, *Psychology of Religion* (London: B. T. Batsford Ltd., 1975), p. 100.

13 Malcolm A. Jeeves, *Psycholocy and Christianity* (Donners Grove, Ill.: Inner varsity Press, 1976), p. 133.

14 Orlo Strunk, Jr., *op. cit.*, p. 63.

15 *Ibid.*, p. 67.

16 *Ibid.*, p. 68.

17 There is practically no research data on the relationship of temperament to religiosity, but Strunk and others believe that temperament plays a significant part in explaining religious experience.

18 Geoffrey E. W. Scobie, *op. cit.*, p. 105.

19 For a more detailed treatment of these examples in Acts cf. Malcolm A. Jeeves, Psychology and Christianity, *op. cit.*, pp. 136-144.

20 Orlo Strunk, Jr., *op. cit.*, p. 86.

21 Geoffrey E. W. Scobie, *Psychology of Religion* (London: B. T. Batsford Ltd., 1975), p. 47.

22 *Ibid.*, p. 52.

23 *Ibid.*, p. 52.

24 *Ibid.*, p. 54.

25 Orlo Strunk, Jr., *op. cit.*, p. 93.

26 *Ibid.*, p. 95.

27 *Ibid.*, p. 97.

28 Paul W. Pruyser, *A Dynamic Psychology of Religion* (New York: Harper and Row Publishers, 1968), p. 176.

29 Orlo Strunk, Jr., *op. cit.*, p. 97.

Chapter Six

Religious Experience

Our Personal Experience

In any discussion of a religious experience we must first determine the phenomenological nature of an experience. Strangely enough the question of the nature and value of an experience arises only when we begin to think of our own experiences. But then, we no longer experience; we think. Once we begin to think of an experience, the experience is passed, for it allows for no self-reflection.. This is the wonder and also the problem in any investigation of experience.

Raimundo Panikkar confronts the problem by comparing the three levels of consciousness that relate a person with reality. These three levels are: the sensuous, the intellectual, and the mystical consciousness. Panikkar describes the three levels as follows:

> The *Sensuous* consciousness relates us by means of our sense organs, to what we could call the material part of reality. The *intellectual* consciousness opens us up to the intelligible world, to that web of relations which give constancy to the material world . . . The *mystical* consciousness identifies us in a very special way to the very reality which it opens up to us.[1]

Ultimately these three levels of consciousness are three dimensions of one and the same primordial consciousness. When we describe a human act as sensory, or intellectual, or mystical we are abstracting i.e. considering but one aspect of a more complex and unified act.

Consciousness in human activity is like a bridge between two shores of reality - the subject and the object. Consciousness connects these two shores of reality by means of one or more of the three levels mentioned. As human beings all of us have consciousness in common, but experience in itself is something particular and personal to each one of us.

Experience as Part of Reality

In conscious activity Panikkar indicates the three stages in which a person integrates himself into reality. In the historical order of human development, Panikkar lists the three moments as: empirical, experimental, and experiential. During the first period of history, the time of the empirical development of human consciousness, the data of the objective world are uncritically accepted and taken as bare facts. The second period is represented by the predominance of experiment. At this point the human being doubts the value of objectivity. Conscious of self as a reflective subject the person takes a more aggressive approach and begins to test the object. It is a period of critical awareness. The experiment is not limited to the object alone; it is also performed on the subject itself. With the advent of experimentation men began to investigate the human mind and all of human reality.

In time human beings lost confidence in mere empirical data, and eventually experimental data seemed too impersonal, too objective. The human consciousness would not be satisfied until the person experiences reality by himself. "The empirical," asserts Panikkar, "is pure objectivity, the experiment blends the object with subjectivity, the experience abolishes any kind of objectivity not assumed and integrated in the subjectivity."[2] As human life developed persons desired individual involvement which can only occur if the experience is there. One cannot experience by proxy. When we consider how different knowing about pain, or love, or God is from experiencing pain, or love, or God we accept the need to appreciate the concept experience in any discussion about religious experience. As we cherish ideas about certain objects (e.g. tree, New York, chair, table etc.) we understand that these ideas can be corrected or modified but always with the appreciation of the distance between us as subjects and the objects under consideration. An experience is different. When we experience pain, we as subjects are one with that idea pain, which touches us. Insofar as it has a primordial or irreducible nature, Panikkar calls it mythical. We cannot go beyond myth as we cannot go beyond experience. Once we explain a myth, it ceases to be such. The same is true of experience.

Panikkar draws the conclusion in the discussion of these three moments in the development of consciousness that any experience may be considered ultimate because experience means immediate contact with reality. To go beyond this is not to excel but to destroy the experience itself. In this sense, any explanation of the experience is less than the experience itself. Perhaps, this admission will help us appreciate better the limits of this entire discussion about religious experience.

Value of Experience

History attests that experiences come and go and do not seem to be lasting. Are there ways of estimating one experience above another? Is it possible that an experience considered valuable today is going to appear tomorrow as utterly untenable? We return to the notion of experience itself. As long as I am having an experience I cannot doubt its existence. Once I wonder about the experience, the experience no longer exists. Thus any self-awareness or judgment about experience is quite different from the experience itself and must be treated in that light.

In an experience the object becomes lost in the subject. The experience is usually short-lived. We as human subjects know that we move back to the realm of reflection and self-consciousness after an experience and recognize ourselves as subjects distinct from the rest of reality. Although in every real experience the object is lost in the subject, the subject itself is never totally lost for it returns into sharp focus when reflection about the experience begins.

If we accept the three degrees of consciousness mentioned earlier, we might distinguish the expression, and interpretation of the experience from the experience itself as correlative to sensory, intellectual and mystical consciousness. The experience in itself would correspond to mystical consciousness in which we acknowledge the ineffability of the real experience. Furthermore, as we distinguish the three stages of consciousness (sensory, intellectual, mystical) we should not lose sight of their underlying unity with the three modes of realization: empirical, experimental and experiential. Basically in our investigation of experience these divisions described by Panikkar should help us not only to distinguish the levels of consciousness but also to understand the ultimate unity of all reality.

An Experience Called Religious

The particular effect of religion upon us stems from our sense of what is generally called a religious experience. The more accepted approach to the study of religious experience is to start not with the historical expression of religion but with the person either as an individual or as a collective or corporate I. Most scientists of religion apply the phenomenological approach, asking: What happens in the experience? What do I observe? Like Paul Tillich, Joachim Wach believes that religious experiences are embedded in general experiences. They are distinguishable but not separated. Wach[3] tells us of four possible views about the nature of a religious experience:

1) There is no such thing

2) Religious experiences occur but they cannot be isolated because they are identical with general experiences.

3) Religious experience can be identified with one historical form of religion itself. (Such is the attitude of some conservative religious group.)

4) Religious experiences occur and can be identified by definite characteristics.

Wach shares this fourth view. He moreover recognizes four characteristics that can be applied to its expression:

1) It is a response to what is experienced as Ultimate Reality.

2) It is a total response of the total being.

3) It is an intense response.

4) It issues in action. (Thus, it involves an imperative.)

(1) Response

As a response it includes four characteristics:

1) Conscious awareness (Panikkar would specify it as nonreflective consciousness.)

2) Part of an encounter

3) Implying a dynamic relationship between experiencer and the experienced

4) Occurring within a particular context that must be accepted, e.g. historical, cultural etc. Therefore it is conditioned. This is most relevant today since the scientific awareness that the Old Testament view of religion is so different from today's experiences.

(2) Total Response

As such, the experience unifies and integrates the person. A true religious experience forces me to be myself as it reveals me to myself in my highest and lowest possibilities.

(3) Intensity

Potentially it is the most powerful, comprehensive, shattering and profound experience of which a person is capable. Since the "gods" transcend the realm of the ordinary, those persons who enter into a relationship with them enter into this life of intensity and deep significance. Many religious leaders in history have manifested this personal sense of intensity in their life-style (e.g. Luther, Wesley, Bernard, Augustine.)

(4) Issues in Action

Action is not to be understood specifically as a contrast to thought or contemplation, but as an opposition to sluggish indifference and inaction.

To Wach as a Western thinker all four characteristics must be present in every religious experience. That implies that there can be no "godless" religion because a full response is needed to another being as a result of dialogue.

Robert B. Marett, Henri Bergson, Brainslaw Malinowski and Raymond Firth are among the chief anthropologists and philosophers of religion who declare that religion is universal in all society.[4] Like Mircea Eliade, Robert Marett suggests we might change the title *homo sapiens* to *homo religiosus*.[5] While the tendency to be religious is inborn, it expresses itself in a wide variety of actions. As man grows he develops his *sensus numinis* through evocation, teaching, and even indoctrination. Applied to Western Christianity: "Christians are not born but made."[6] William Ralph Inge claims that true religion is not taught but caught from someone who already has it.[7] All major religions provide an atmosphere for divine instruction and spiritual growth. This leads us to the question of the object of religious experience, the Ultimate Reality. If *finitum non capax infiniti*, how can we have any knowledge of Ultimate Reality as the object of our religious experience? It is Jewish and

Christian theology that responds by telling us that God or Ultimate Reality manifests itself in an encounter called revelation. As such God is not known simply as an object but as a personal being experienced in a relationship of an encounter or dialogue. God initiates the dialogue and convinces us that he is personal and alive and interested in involving himself in our personal life. Various religions show their differences by the way they explain the media of revelation. William Temple in *Nature, Man, and God* succinctly describes the Christian idea of revelation:

> We affirm, then, that unless all existence is a medium of Revelation, no particular Revelation is possible; for the possibility of Revelation depends on the personal quality of that supreme and ultimate Reality which is God. If there is no Ultimate Reality, which is the ground of all else, then there is no God to be revealed; if that Reality is not personal, there can be no special revelation, but only uniform procedure; . . .[8]

Thus a religious experience must account for these elements: revelation, an object revealing, and a subject aware of some sort of revelation. The entire experience centers itself on the idea of a relationship established, not knowledge communicated. Since human beings are distinct, each receives Ultimate Reality differently. In Western religions it is assumed that this revelation or relationship is open to all persons, that is, it is universal.

How truth is portrayed in religion becomes most engaging for the outside observer. In the religious experience the finite becomes bound up in the infinite and the infinite in the finite. In Christianity, as in Hinduism and Buddhism, the divine goes so far as to adapt itself to human forms.[9] Joachim Wach describes this apprehension of Ultimate Reality under three aspects: mystery, spontaneity and majesty.[10] In considering the Ultimate Reality as *mysterium* or mystery we do not mean it is so foreign to man as to be wholly other. In a numinous, or mysterious way the infinite reaches us through finite mediation in time and space (i.e. history).

The second aspect under which Ultimate Reality manifests itself is that of spontaneity or creativity. In a religious experience Ultimate Reality is alive and dynamic. For Jews and Christians the revelational experience is dynamic because God is living and man is living. Modern metaphysics represented by Bergson, Whitehead and Hartshorne turns toward a dynamic, ongoing conception of Ultimate Reality rather than a static immutable conception.

The third aspect under which Ultimate Reality manifests itself is majesty or power. Wach points out that in most religions the majesty of God is given powerful expression. He quotes Lewis Farnell who says: "In Vedic and Vedantic theology, in Hellenic, the Judaic, the Christian, the Islamic, and the Zarathustrian system, the multiplicity of divine attributes should be brought under the three great categories Potentia, Sapientia, Bonitas - Power, Wisdom and Goodness."[11]

The Subject of Religious Experience

With an understanding of the three characteristics of Ultimate Reality touching the mind of the person engaged in a religious experience, Joachim Wach turns to the analysis of the subjective factor in a religious experience. Like Rudolf Otto, Wach declares that there can be no genuine religious experience unless the person has a sense of awe (tremendum) but not to the exclusion of attraction (fascinosum).[12] The latter plays a major role in Hinduism, Buddhism and Christianity.

Insofar as Ultimate Reality creates a sense of awe and attraction in the subject, the subject has some cognitive awareness of the Ultimate Reality. As stated earlier Ultimate Reality is not known like things are known; rather it is understood only in the act of encounter. As in every human encounter, the knowledge of the person encountered is deeper, more mysterious and puzzling, more challenging than the knowledge that comes from knowing a material "thing."

Context of Religious Experience

Religious experience occurs in concrete situations.[13] A person living in space and time engages in conscious communication with that which transcends space and time. Some forms of religion stress a detachment from physical life, but the physical context of religious experience cannot be denied. The whole person - body and soul - is involved in a religious experience. The concrete historical world is the constant condition of this religious reality. Recently, the excessive spiritualistic (idealistic) interpretations of religious experience have been counterbalanced by the sociological investigation of societal factors in religious motivation. Scholars like Max Weber, Ernst Troeltsch and Max Scheler have paved the way for greater sensitivity to these more concrete elements in religion.

Subject Versus Organization

Abraham Maslow found in the history of many religions a tendency to develop two extreme wings:

a) The "mystical" and individual on one hand,
b) The legalistic and organizational on the other.

The authentically religious person is able to integrate these trends automatically, but he is never reduced to the organizational dimensions of religion. Many religious people however allow organized religion to become enemies to personal religious experiences and the experiencer. That is the main thesis of Maslow's work, *Religions, Values and Peak-Experiences*. Rather than define a peak experience Maslow leads up to the term by distinguishing the plateau experience from the peak experience. The plateau experience can be achieved, earned, and learned, and often extends over a period of time. The peak experience by contrast is not voluntary; it carries with it the elements of surprise and wonder.

Every known revealed or "high" religion has been founded through the personal revelation and illumination coming to some acutely sensitive prophet or seer. Each of these revealed religions exists on the communication and codification of this original mystic experience or revelation from the lonely prophet to the mass of beings in general. For Maslow these revelations can be subsumed under the title of "peak experiences" or "ecstasies." What was formerly considered supernatural and limited to a few Maslow contends should be treated as natural and capable of being received by many. In fact, as his investigations continued he discovered more and more people were able to describe peak experiences. The "non-peakers" by contrast were simply those who were afraid of having a "peak experience." The completely mechanistic, materialistic or practical person who tends to be means-oriented avoids such experiences since they "earn no money, bake no bread, chop no wood."[14]

In the past organized religion was considered to be an effort to communicate peak experiences to non-peakers. Eventually the ceremonies, symbols, rules and credal formulas became the substance of religion instead of the original revelation given to the religious leaders. To make matters worse, the task of handing on religion often fell into the hands of the non-peakers. Religious expression soon was divided between the mystic, "peakers" or privately religious people on one hand, and the organization men, or non-peakers on the other. Thus, instead of several main-line religions Maslow sees only two religions in the world: the religion of the peakers and that of the non-peakers, or those who accept the joy and challenge of a religious experience and those who repress or suppress them and therefore cannot make use of religion for their personal growth.

In the past the organization of religion tended to create the impression that a religious experience (peak experience) is rare. Maslow contends that when we are normal, and healthy, and adequately fulfilling the concept of "human being," religious experiences and experiences of transcendence should in principle be commonplace.[15]

Maslow's Survey

In 270 personal and written interviews Abraham Maslow sifted reports of what people considered their "peak experiences." In his question put to the candidates he stated: "I would like you to think of the most wonderful experience or experiences of your life: happiest moments, ecstatic moments, moments of rapture . . . First list these. And then try to tell how you feel in such acute moments."[16] Maslow found that practically everything that was recounted in the peak-experiences naturalistic though they are, could be listed under the heading of religious happening or religious experience.

What follows is a description of these experiences based on his findings:[17]

1) First, it is quite characteristic in peak-experiences that the subject perceives the entire universe as an integrated or unified whole. In this perception there is a sense of belonging, a sense of being integrated with the whole of reality. For some people this is the basic meaning of religious faith.

2) The event can best be described as non-evaluating, non-comparing or non-judging cognition. Thus, important and unimportant are not differentiated. (Panikkar would describe it as non-reflective activity).

3) The subject sees the world and individual persons as more detached from human concerns. Detachment and objectivity characterize this experience.

4) As a consequence, the event is more object-centered than ego-centered.

5) The event is felt as highly valuable - even uniquely valuable. In fact, peak experiences can make all of life worthwhile by their occasional occurrence.

6) As a consequence to No. 5, these experiences are seen as end-experiences and not mere means-experiences.

7) In the experience there is a disorientation of time and space, or even a lack of consciousness of time and space. In a positive way the subject has a feeling of universality and eternity.

8) The world in a peak-experience is seen only as beautiful, good, desirable, worthwhile, etc. . . . The world is accepted. The subject seems to understand it. Somehow he becomes reconciled to the evil that is a part of the whole. Although the questionnaire called for a report of the most blissful and happy moments of life, there is a recognition that in these moments the bad things in life are accepted more totally than they are in other times.

9) Consequently, in becoming "godlike" the "gods" who encompass the whole of being see it as good, and just. Evil, however, is a product of limited or selfish vision.

10) The general description of peak-moments corresponds with what people through the ages call the eternal verities, or the spiritual values, or the highest values.

11) B- cognition, or knowledge of being (a Maslow term) in a peak experience is much more passive and receptive than normal perception is.

12) Emotions like: wonder, awe, reverence, surrender are frequently described.

13) In peak experiences the dichotomies, polarities, and conflicts of life are transcended or resolved. The person tends to move toward integration, fusion, and unity of apparent opposites. (Cf. No. 2.)

14) There tends to be a loss of: fear, anxiety, inhibition, defense and control.

15) Peak-experiences often have profound after effects upon a person, somewhat like a religious conversation (e.g. John Wesley). Lesser effects could be called therapeutic.

16) In a naturalistic way, it is like visiting heaven and returning to tell about it.

17) There is a tendency to move more closely to a perfect identity or understanding of one's real self.

18) The person feels more free, more the center of his own perceptions and activities.

19) Also, with a sharper identity one is better able to transcend his "ego" and become selfless.

20) The peak-experiencer becomes more loving and more accepting and thus he becomes more spontaneous, honest, and innocent.

21) He becomes less an object, more a person, more subject to psychological laws opening up the "higher life."

22) Like No. 19, he becomes less selfish, more selfless, more godlike.

23) A feeling of fortune and luck follows a peak experience. A common reaction is: "I don't deserve this."

24) The dichotomy between humility and pride tends to be resolved. Both are fused into a single complex subordinate unity.

25) The sense of the sacred penetrates the secular and worldly. (Cf. No. 13, 1).

All attempts to appreciate religious experiences must include an examination of ourselves as persons. When I look at reality, I must reflect that I am an active interacting part of reality. I stand in awe of experiences like a Montana sunset only to discover progressively that I am a part of the experience, that I am one with the sunset. As Panikkar contends, I do not reflect during the experience, but when it is over and relegated to the recesses of my memory I reflect upon the transcendence of the event, the sunset and my understanding of my relation to the sunset. Somehow my transcendence enables me to personally experience the basic unity of life. In this experience I go beyond the limits of my day to day reaction to reality.

When I admit my experiences I move to confirm them and to allow them to enter my total being. Although these experiences are awesome and often puzzling I believe in them. This psychological faith William Kraft defines "as a creative acceptance or admittance of experiences that cannot be explained."[18] As difficult as they are to explain to myself and others they are real and are known by me prereflectively. Human psychological faith comes from my innermost being. In faith I accept or reject my experiences. When I choose to accept reality and its mystery I affirm my experience. "Faith means," says Kraft, "that I will continue to follow reality and consequently become a disciple of mystery."[19] As we mature we become more realistic about our demands on life and its mysteries. We learn to appreciate reality as in process. Absolute certainty is impossible because it is against the emergent nature of reality. Thus authentic human faith is a matter of personal growth and development not simply a matter of having a system of justifying the unknown.

Kraft's Survey

Like Abraham Maslow, William Kraft interviewed scores of people who claimed to have experiences of God or Ultimate Reality. He found that each person's experience of "God" differed somewhat from another's.[20] Factors such as religion, education, ethnic background and personal history influenced a person's experience of the Ultimate. Yet, he found certain dominant characteristics in his research. Although people used various terms in talking of their religious experiences such as: God, Absolute Thou, ultimate concern and Personal Transcendent, all were pointing to the same reality.[21] William Kraft found specific characteristics showing up again and again as people related their religious experiences. The following is a descriptive analysis of eight of the major common characteristics found in Kraft's research. The eight characteristics are: mystery, dependence,, indebtedness, faith and doubt, love expressed in worship, transcendence, holiness, and unity.

Mystery

Like all "self" experiences (i.e. self as distinguished from the ego and the body) a religious experience involves mystery. Poetic and mystical terms are often employed in an attempt to describe adequately what is in reality quite mysterious. Although this holy experience is beyond ready analysis, it points to a lived and undeniable experience. The normal world of dichotomies, paradoxes, and day to day problems fades into the background in comparison with the strangely attractive religious experience. Yet how do I regard this phenomenon? Eventually I realize with Joachim Wach that my sacred experience is related integrally with my day to day profane experiences. In my transcendence I unite the two types by contrast, comparison, and synthesis of relevant real experiences. Meanwhile mystery stands in the background as a faithful and attentive sentinal.

Dependence

A second characteristic of a religious experience communicated by a variety of respondents is a sense of dependence. I depend on the Other because I need the Other in my total understanding of reality and also I love the Other. I acknowledge that the Holy Other is a greater and more sacred reality than myself. The Other is the very ground of my existence. Consequently, my respect for the Other is spontaneous and meaningful and gives meaning to all reality around me.

This dependence on the holy is unique. It is not a childish, immature, or short-sighted dependence rooted in my own weakness.

Rather it is a dependence of openness and concern for my position in relation to the Other and the rest of the Universe. It is a responsible dependence, centered on giving. It is a dependence that renders me personally dependable.

Indebtedness

As I grow to maturity my openness to life allows me to respond to the gifts bestowed on me by the Other. After a religious experience I fall captive to a primordial mood of indebtedness. I reflect that I owe the Other everything - my life, my existence, my future. In return I want to give myself to the Other. If I and others do not return the gift of ourselves to the Other by giving to each other, life and society will deteriorate. William Kraft remarks, "When people never give of themselves, the culture suffers and becomes a culture of things, not of persons."[22]

In my indebtedness I realize the Other makes demands on me only in terms of appeal not force. The Other invites me to do nothing more than love. Paradoxically the more I pay my debt to the Other, the more I owe, because the more I give to the Other the more the Other returns to me. Kraft remarks, "my degree of indebtedness is indicative of my degree of holiness."[23]

Faith and Doubt

Before, during and after a religious experience a paradoxical unity of faith and doubt are present. My faith does not produce certainty; it enlightens the mystery of the Other, but doubt remains. Indeed a life without doubt is sheer fantasy. Meanwhile faith makes sense out of my experience, modifies my uncertainty, and allows doubt to function at critical moments of questioning. My faith fills out the reality of my religious experiences while doubt functions as an active questioner of the other.

Love Expressed in Worship

The singular nature of love prompts the experiencers to worship the Other. In religion one often finds mere ritual indications of worship, but authentic worship accepts the inviting power of the Other and responds to this love by love. The mode of worship is a separate issue. When his everyday life is lived in the context of love, a religious person finds that it becomes a subtle yet constant ever present worship of the Other.

Transcendence

In my religious experiences I live beyond my usual modes of interaction. In my experiences of the Other I move to an intimate union with the mystery of all reality. In this way I transcend myself only to find a fuller picture of reality. My transcendence is acknowledged as very human, lived in the concrete and crucial experiences of each day. The joy of transcendence includes the clear realization of my own limits and my unique human ability to go beyond my limits as I do in a religious experience. I am at one with reality as I experience the power to go beyond my normal human limits. With this experience I can honor and promote the Other as my ultimate concern and ground of all reality.

Holiness

Every person operates according to a hierarchy of values, and each person has an ultimate value - that is, a standard, activity or object which he values most. Holiness can be described as what I value most and upon which I base my life. Insofar as this value functions as the greatest influence in my life, it is sacred.

"The authentic lover," says Kraft, "always participates explicitly or implicitly in the sacredness of the Other."[24] The human other or Ultimate Other is made sacred in love. Each authentic love experience therefore is a sacred experience because both participants come to experience the sacred basis of their love. Admitting the different levels of sacredness only the experience of the Other is fully sacred.

Unity

As a person experiences the Holy Other in reciprocal love, there is also an experience of a certain unity with the Other, and with the universe. As I experience the world, even before I reflect upon it I experience a harmony and unity rooted in the Holy Other. Tensions, problems, questions that arise in my growth process do not take away from this sense of unity. Thus, contrary to uninformed attitudes, a person who has religious experiences is very much in tune with reality. The person becomes holy in experiencing the Holy, and in living this holiness shows a healthy and mature disposition to others as part of this experience of the Other. A holy person says yes to the holiness and wholeness of human growth and self-emergence. Once a person chooses to be open in love to the manifestations of the Other, he begins to realize who he is, and what he is in his orientation to the Other.

The Experience of No-thingness

One experience that is normal, perhaps even necessary, for a holy life is the experience of no-thingness. William Kraft describes no-thingness as an experience at certain stages in a person's maturity "when the world and others recede into the background leaving me with myself in the foreground."[25] In effect, no-thingness is a gift of self-confrontation. I come face to face with myself. The heart of my existence is thrown into focus demanding that I take stock of myself.

In no-thingness I am lonely. Paradoxically, I feel the presence of the Other in his absence. My faith in the Other is not necessarily affected. It may, in fact, become strengthened. I miss people and want to be with them, but for various reasons I am unable to fulfill my desire. Similar to the experience of physical illness, I withdraw from the Other and others only to find myself needing the Other and others to alleviate my suffering. I am caught in the paradox of desiring to be alone and simultaneously calling out for care. This loneliness of no-thingness permeates every fiber of my existence. The Other and others are there in reality but I cannot reach them. Likewise I have the distinct feeling they cannot reach me. The pain of self-confrontation in no-thingness is acute, but progressively it lessens preparing me for the joy of one day being with others.

I cannot will to be lonely but I can will to be alone. Aloneness often increases the possibility of being lonely by decreasing defenses against loneliness. But a healthy aloneness is an aid to life-emergence. Healthy aloneness is solitude - chosen for the purpose of self-exploration, meditation, study, enjoyment, listening, or simply "being." One of the most significant acts of solitude explains Kraft, "is to do nothing."[26] Choosing to be alone for the right reasons means creative discovery and growth. Indeed, healthy living seeks to provide certain times for aloneness in solitude whether this be for doing things or for "no-thing."

Whatever the course, or circumstances, when I am in the state of no-thingness Kraft contends "I am thrown back on myself - my existence is "depressed."[27] I am depressed because I feel that I am losing the ground for my existence. I feel lost in my nothingness. Psychologically distant from the world of things and people I am "pressed in" on myself. A world of history and values, once so familiar, suddenly disappears leaving me with no-thing to grasp.

My striving to make sense out of things makes me anxious and frustrated resulting in the powerful realization that I am in the middle of no-thing. I am lost in the middle of nothingness with nowhere to go. Once again I examine the ground of my existence and wonder about the possibility of any future to my life. By way of support Kraft remarks:

> These experiences are often painful but necessary and healthy for deeper growth into life, because loneliness, solitude, withdrawal, depression, emptiness, guilt, frustration, anxiety, and dread in no-thingness lead to self expression for life. Although I stand in anxiety on the precarious ground of no-thingness, my anxious pain in no-thingness prepares me to be with and for the Other. In no-thingness I discover transcendent meaning and the freedom

to dwell in and to enjoy the world. Paradoxically my suffering enables me to say yes to life.[28]

Thus, sense emerges from apparent non-sense, meaning from suffering and meaninglessness. I return to the real world and see all in balance. I confront the basic limit of human living that when I decide to move in one direction I cannot go likewise in another. It hurts to learn my limits but it hurts more to live in a fantasy world where there are no limits and to make decisions accordingly.

Having experienced no-thingness I am more sensitive to myself and others. I have learned that the more I am in tune with myself, the more I am in tune with others. I find that growth in knowing myself is the most fundamental form of creativity and that it serves as the basis for all other forms of creativity. Kraft comments:

In no-thingness I realize that no one can give me freedom or make me healthy. I discover that I must earn my authenticity by learning and living the meaning of authentic dependency, independency, and interdependency. I admit that these projects are my responsibility and that although others influence and help me, no one except me can live my life.[29]

After I have lived through nothingness I am prepared to experience the Holy (to be aware of a religious experience). While not a guarantee that religious experiences will follow, my experience of no-thingness reminds me of my availability to the Holy Other. As a positive support Kraft points out that self-confrontation in no-thingness is a normal prelude for the experience of the Other. In no-thingness we are freed to experience the love of the Other. A direct experience of no-thingness can occur at any time, but Kraft points out that his experience is more likely to occur at certain stages in life such as: early adolescence, late adolescence, adulthood, middle-age, old age and just before death. All the stages of no-thingness are basically the same; however the experience has particular significance according to issues involved in self-confrontation at a particular state in human growth.[30]

The sense of no-thingness is dramatic and eerie in its realization. To find myself in a position whereby I must look into myself for my own good strikes me as strangely difficult, and serious, but not destructive, or disastrous. Eventually, I can look to this possibility of experiencing nothingness with hope and optimism.

Reflection Upon Religious Experience

The position of religious experience in the total picture of religion is subject to various interpretations by scholars and students of the subject. As we continue our investigation of the role of the individual and the community in a religious experience we should attempt to fathom the understanding of reality that flows from a religious experience.

After a person has an experience, he tends to communicate this experience to the rest of society by means of language. In the normal course of events knowledge of the world is built up in society by means of this communication. Rem Edwards[31] discusses two theories of perceptual experience applicable to religious experience - the building block theory and the matrix theory.

Building Block Theory

In the building block theory of perception we bring nothing to the experience. Everything that we perceive and come to believe about reality is constructed out of our encounter with "Ultimate Reality." Religious experience among the varieties of experience is the beginning and end of all religious knowledge. What ultimately matters is our immediate acquaintance with God in religious experience.

In the 1920's and 1930's philosophers like Bertrand Russell, Ludwig Wittgenstein and Rudolf Carnap advocated that we construct an ideal language that would be free of all the defects and misleading implications of natural languages. Perceptual experiences would provide information about the three basic items in the universe for this ideal language: individuals, qualities, and relations. As our experience of these materials builds up we can become more confident of our understanding of the world. The

names of individuals, qualities and relations become the building
blocks of our ideal language in time combining with one another to
form more complex linguistic units.

For theologians like Buber, Brunner and Baillie[32] the religious
experience should be so clear and self-explanatory that on it an entire religious world view could be built. However, what they stress
is the personal value of such an experience. Subsequent language
and propositions are of importance only insofar as it is fitting that
religious belief be communicated to society as a whole.

The Matrix Theory

The basic idea of the matrix theory is that all experience occurs
within a given matrix of beliefs, perceptions, and interpretations.
While it is true that experience modifies the matrix, it is also true
that the matrix provides an indispensible context for interpreting
the experience and for assessing its truthfulness. Realistically the
matrix could exert a power that modifies the quality of the experience itself. The proponents of this theory rooted in the writings of
Charles Sanders Peirce and Alfred North Whitehead consider it
impossible to interpret any type of experience without a language
since interpretation is a function of a language.[33]

Suppose I have the experience of a yellow candle. In reflecting
upon it I say "I see a yellow candle there." All of the words presup-
pose distinctions based on preconceptions and preknowledge: I, a
pronoun, distinct from other pronouns, yellow as distinct from
other colors, candle as distinct from other objects, there as distinct
from here. Without previous distinctions developed into a language form I would be unable to interpret this particular experience. By contrast, the proponents of the building block theory are
hard pressed to give examples of pure, self-sufficient, self-inter-
preting reports of evidence.

Thus in the matrix theory we approach any experience with a
ready made language and a ready made set of beliefs, but experience is still the best teacher. Scientists agree that the man who has
no preconceived theories and hypotheses to test is the man who is

least likely to learn from experience.[34] Moreover, when we inquire how we differentiate between a true or "veridical" experience and one that is illusory, we find that we cannot tell the difference between the two unless we already know what is real and what is unreal. Only with preconceptions about what is real and what is unreal do we know what experience to trust.[35]

The Reliability of Private Experience

In determining what is real and what is unreal through preconceptions we can state that objective reality is what can be experienced publicly by many of us. Subjective reality is what one or only a few experience. In standard empiricist terms, "veridical" experiences (real experiences) are those we share with other people, whereas illusions and hallucinations (unreal experiences) are experiences that are private and unshared.[36] Only if other minds exist and interact can we tell the difference between real and non-real experiences. Hence, empiricism presupposes metaphysical pluralistic personalism. Unless I trust what others say about their experiences, I cannot determine that my experience of their external physical behaviour is not an illusion or hallucination. No single item of experience stands on its own. Private experience is a part of all sorts of shared experiences even if it does not move to verification by sharing. (Who the normal observers are that bring objective reality to an experience is yet another question we will not pursue here). Basically, it is not the experience that is true or false, it is our interpretations of it. When we enter the field of interpretation we must admit that no interpretation stands on its own (howsoever private the experience may be). Each interpretation stands or falls with the entire world view and must be tested in part by its consistency with our interpretation of other experiences and ultimately with all that we believe.[37]

Utilizing the principles of the matrix theory we might inquire how a religious experience might enter into the construction of a religious world view. If a religious experience occurs within a matrix of beliefs, preconceptions, and interpretations and if the experience may modify the matrix, it is also true that the matrix provides an indispensible context for interpreting the experience and for assessing its veracity. Just as it is impossible to build a scientific world view upon pure sense experience, so it is impossible to build a religious world view out of pure religious experience. Nevertheless there is a learning and development that arises from a religious experience much like that which occurs in the experience of a scientist who is already armed with preconceived theories and hypotheses in need of testing. Rem Edwards says: "The man who is most likely to find God in a religious experience is the man who already has some conception of God and to some extent knows what he is looking for."[38]

Admittedly there is a danger that the interpreter of the experience will read his preconceptions into the experience, but that danger is one that the interpreter of religious experience shares with the scientist as he interprets his sense experience. All that we can expect is that both be open to experience, willing to learn from it and to modify their preconceptions in the light of it. Religious people should compare notes just as scientists do. There is a community of religious believers just as there is a community of scientific believers. Again we state that the interpretation of any experience is only as strong as the entire world view within which it is set.

Comparing the statements made by religious experiences of various times, races and religions, we find a common basis as well as great differences in detail. For C. D. Broad[39] it is obvious that the interpretations depend in a large measure on the traditional religious beliefs in which various experiencers have been raised. A feeling of undifferentiated unity with the rest of the universe will be interpreted by a Christian who believes in a personal God quite differently from a Hindu mystic who has been trained in a different metaphysical tradition. The relations between the experiences and the traditional beliefs of the experiencers are quite complex. The beliefs and traditions alonng with the expectations we highlight largely determine what interpretation we shall put on a certain sensation or experience. Moreover, these beliefs, traditions, and expectations do to some extent modify the sensible characteristics of the experience itself. With an ever growing complexity beliefs affect and determine experiences, but experiences likewise affect beliefs. In time beliefs become traditions only to affect the religious experiences at a deeper level.

Revelation

In Western society, those who claim they have an experience of the object of their religion understand this experience often under the category of revelation. John Macquarrie[40] describes the cognitive element in this experience while cautioning the reader not to isolate this element from the total understanding of religious experience involving object and subject in dialogue. The word revelation in its root meaning suggests an unveiling of what hitherto has been hidden. The Greek word for truth (aletheia) means unhiddenness implying that its discovery is always an experience of unveiling or revealing. We attain truth when that which was concealed or hidden is brought out into the light.

The theological conception of revelation is of a different order from the ordinary knowing experiences in life. Thus, when recipients of revelatory experiences try to describe them, they must stretch ordinary language beyond the limits of normal usage to the point of seeming to use fantastic expressions to describe to us the unusual experiences of the "holy" breaking into their life. Nevertheless, a definite pattern runs throughout the basic description of all revelation. Whether it is the revelation granted to Moses in the desert or John on an island there is a mood of meditation in face of the sudden in-breaking of the "holy."

What is described as revelation has much in common with what we have described as religious experience. Revelation is a mode of religious experience when our estimate of religious experience focuses on judging, assisting, or addressing. Thus, unable to draw a clear line between religious experience and revelation, we distinguish the two in the light of the theological goals of a given discussion. In practice when one accepts a special experience as a religious experience, he need not proceed further to determine the way in which the "holy other" or Ultimate Reality was revealed to him. This *post factum* reflection is valuable for the individual person but we must return to the principle that no theology as such is founded on private revelation since theology expresses the faith of the community. Classic revelation implies a disclosure of the "holy" to the founder of the community. This disclosure becomes the model for subsequent experiences of the "Holy Other" in that community.[41] In sum, revelation is a concern of the whole community, while a religious experience is tied to individual persons. However, revelation occurs in connection with a religious experience.

Three Levels of Thinking

Drawing from the philosophy of Martin Heidegger, John Macquarrie develops an epistemology of revelation by asking how we come to know what is revealed after the fact. First of all, Macquarrie distinguishes three levels of thinking beginning with calculative thinking.*

By far the commonest mode of thinking, calculative thinking provides a subject-object pattern. What we think about we consider as an "object" to us, set over against us and outside of us. We direct our thinking towards handling, using, and manipulating this object. The typical development of this thinking shows up in the fields of science or technology.

The second level of thinking Macquarrie designates is "existential" thinking. Also common to every day existence this mode of thinking recognizes what is thought about as another subject, having the same kind of being as the person who does the thinking. Thus, this kind of thinking involves participation in the existence of the other subject that is thought about. One special case of existential thinking for our discussion of revelation is what we call "repetitive" thinking. More than a mechanical "repeating" this type of thinking implies going into some experience that has been handed down in such a way that it is brought into the present and its insights are made alive again. Historical happenings, or documents such as poems or narratives (e.g. the Bible) handed down from the past are practical examples of "repetitive" thinking. To "get into" the happening or document we must think with the agent or the author.

Another form of existential thinking is personal knowledge. In an "I-thou" relationship each thinks of the other as subject. However, I can know the other person only insofar as he makes himself known i.e. insofar as he "reveals" himself to me. In a truly personal knowledge we do not subject the other to us, but we meet the subject on a footing of mutuality and reciprocity. One might hasten to compare revelation of God to man as an "I-thou" type of meeting. In a revelatory experience, the idea of I-thou is only analogous because the person who receives the revelation is utterly transcended by the holy being who reveals himself. This one-sidedness implies that a personal encounter with "Ultimate Reality" could only be a very remote analogue.[42] Moreover, the meeting between man and Ultimate Reality is not a typical physical meeting of persons. Satisfaction that one knows the "Other" is not attained. However, this does not mean that we should cease to consider the meeting of God and man in revelation as anything less than a dialogue.

After considering the subject-object mode of thinking and the subject-subject mode, Macquarrie presents a third possibility. In this mode I would be subjected to that which is known to the extent that I am transcended, mastered and known myself. He calls this mode "primordial" or essential thinking. In contrast to the other two modes involving probing and calculating, this mode has a meditative character that waits and listens. In keeping with our idea of revelation as dialogue, this third mode responds to the address of the "being" or the "Other." As such, it links the primordial thinking of the philosopher with the revelatory experience of the religious person. What is known is not another being but being itself, a being as Macquarrie states, "that communicates itself through all the particular beings by which it is present, by which it manifests itself, and not least through the depth of our being, for we too are participants in being."[43] Thus, in addition to an understanding of religious experience, Macquarrie helps us to appreciate the type of revelation that comes out of the experience and sustains us in our religious life.

Knowledge flowing from primordial thinking has a giftlike character. Being grasps the recipient rather than the recipient grasps being, yet the recipient is not completely overwhelmed by being. In a religious experience, the somewhat overwhelming giftlike character of being carries the two very significant ideas of *tremendum* and *fascinans* (as Otto points out). We stand in the grace and openness of being that reveals itself not only in otherness (I-thou dialogue) but also in kinship, so that even as we are grasped by being revealing itself we also grasp being and hold on to it.

John Macquarrie believes that a genuinely primordial "thinking" or primordial experience of the revelation of being is rare. "For most of us," he says, "there can be only the repetitive thinking that follows in the course of some classic experience of the holy, as that experience has come down to us in a concrete symbolism, and as it has subsequently been lit up further by generations of thought and experience in the community of faith which it founded."[44]

Mystical Experience

In any discussion of religious experience we come across the expression "mystical experience" or "mystical consciousness." When we raise the question "What is mysticism?" we really mean "What is a mystical experience?" Immediately we add: "Is a mystical experience the same as a religious experience?" Walter Stace[45] believes there are several reasons for insisting that a mystical experience in itself is not a religious phenomenon. If we strip the mystical experience of all intellectual interpretation, what is left is simply the sense of undifferentiated unity. The idea of religion enters the picture only when the experiencer interprets what he means by this undifferentiated unity. In theistic religion of the West (Judaism, Islam, Christianity, and Zoroastrianism) this experience of undifferentiated unity is interpreted as union with God. Moreover,

Christian mystics like Eckhart and Ruysbroeck interpret undifferentiated unity in terms of a Trinitarian conception of God.[46] Islamic mystics interpret it as the unitarian God of Islam. Vedantists interpret it as more impersonal absolute. Buddhists interpret it as a Void or Nirvana. (By denying the existence of a Supreme Being Buddhists present the possibility of an atheistic mystical experience). Yet, in spite of its variety of descriptions why does mysticism usually take on some religious form? Walter Stace[47] offers three reasons: First, in a typical introvertive mystical experience there is a sense of melting away into the infinite of one's own individuality. The same phases such as "melting away" or "fading away" are found in the mystical literature of Christianity, Islam, Hinduism, and Buddhism.

The second reason for a connection between mysticism and religion is that the "undifferentiated unity" is necessarily thought of by the mystics as being beyond space and time. Being timeless is the same as being eternal, and in religious minds the eternal like the infinite is another name of God. Thus, the mystical experience is thought of as an experience of God.

The third reason for the identification of undifferentiated unity with religion lies in the emotional side of the experience. Mystics contend that their experience brings feelings of peace, blessedness, and joy. It becomes identified with the peace of God, the entrance to divinity and salvation. In Buddhism this experience becomes Nirvana and as such is identified with the supreme goal of the Buddhist religious life. Thus, mysticism naturally, though not necessarily becomes intimately associated with whatever is religious of the culture in which it appears. Mystical experiences in themselves do not tend to make a person a Christian or a Buddhist. Nevertheless the experiencer is likely to feel that in the particular religious experience he has found something sacred. This sense of the sacred may be enough to change his life, and to give it new meaning and value. Should this occur, the sociologist reminds us that this person is acting religiously.

Mystical Consciousness

Mystical consciousness is different from rational consciousness which operates on the level of sensations, thoughts, and concepts. Mystical consciousness (or experience in Panikkar's sense of the term) contains no sensations, thoughts, or concepts. For this reason mystics usually say their experience are ineffable. The mystic often attempts a reflective description of the experience, but at best this description proves inadequate. Mystical experiences simply cannot be measured. Thus, any visions, voices, telepathy, precognition, or clairvoyance cannot be lumped together into the category of mystical experience. Once the sensory-intellectual consciousness is operative, the experience is not mystical. Although mystical consciousness is rare it is not miraculous. "Owing to the comparative rarity of this kind of consciousness, it should no doubt," says Walter Stace, "be assigned to the sphere of abnormal psychology."[48]

Types of Mysticism

Allowing that mystical experiences have different characteristics in different ages, there is nevertheless one characteristic common to all. In the final analysis each mystical experience involves the apprehension of an ultimate nonsensuous unity in all things.[49] In other words, this experience completely transcends our sensory-intellectual consciousness. Within this basic mystical experience there are two main types. One may be called the extrovertive type, the other introvertive. Both apprehend the "one" but they reach it in different ways. The extrovertive type looks outward and through the physical senses into the external world and finds the one there. The introvertive type by contrast turns inward and finds the one at the bottom of the self, at the base of the human personality. Walter Stace reminds us that the introvertive type is the more common strand in the history of mysticism.[50] The Catholic mystic, Meister Eckhart (c. 1260-1329), one dramatic example of the extrovertive type, wrote, "Here (i.e. in this experience) all blades of grass, wood and stone, all things are one . . . When is a man in mere understanding? When he sees one thing separated from another. And when is he above mere understanding? When he sees all in all, then a man stands above mere understanding."[51] Americans can readily call to mind the poetry of Walt Whitmann expressed in similar terms. In the writings of both, the extrovertive understanding retains in some delicate manner the distinctions between things in the unity. The grass becomes identified with the stone, but somehow it also retains its own identity.

The introvertive mystic attempts to suppress the whole empirical content of consciousness. Actually, not all consciousness disappears but only the ordinary sensory-intellectual consciousness disappears and is replaced by the mystical consciousness.

Admittedly, it is most difficult to stop all sensing, imagining, and thinking by a determined act of the will. Nevertheless, the mystic attempts to do just that. The mystics may employ various methods to achieve this new consciousness. For example, there are the Yoga techniques of India, the concentration on a single point in consciousness by a repetition of a verbal formula, and a concentrated uprooting of all desires. Although mystics avoid direct references to themselves, eventually they become aware of mystical consciousness as a feeling of ineffable peace, the Supreme Good, the Self alone. The core of the experience is simply a oneness, or undifferentiated unity, a pure consciousness bathed in paradox. Indeed there is pure peace, beatitude, joy, which Buddhists call Nirvana, but there is also a void, a nothingness. That is the negative side of the paradox, not as in the Johannine expression: "a light shining in the darkness," but more pointedly, a light that is darkness. Once again we ask if mysticism is wholly subjective or whether it actually points to some reality outside the experiencer's mind? Should we be forced to limit its identity to the subjective consciousness, at least we see it as a value supremely enriching human life. In this sense it stands in strength and stability by itself.

An Outsider's View

How does an "outsider" make a reasonable assessment of the possibility of a religious experience when he feels he has never had such an experience? When we discover that there are certain experiences that occur at all times and places although only infrequently with any high degree of intensity and not among all persons, and when the experiences involve certain basic conditions which are common to them, two alternatives are open to us: 1) we may suppppose that these persons are in contact with an aspect of reality which is not revealed to ordinary persons in their everyday experience or 2) we may suppose that these persons are all subject to a delusion from which other men are free. C. D. Broad[52] introduces three analogous cases to illustrate our confrontation with these two alternatives. Two of the cases are real and a third is imaginary.

Case No. 1

Most of the detailed facts which biologists tell us about the minute structure and changes in cells can be perceived only by persons who have had a long training in the use of a microscope. In this first case we notice that the agreement among trained microscopists really does correspond to facts which untrained persons cannot perceive.

Case No. 2

Persons of all cultures who habitually drink alcoholic beverages to excess eventually have perceptual experiences in which they seem to themselves to see pink rats and snakes crawling about their rooms. In this case we believe that the agreement among drunkards is merely a uniform hallucination.

Case No. 3

Imagine a race of human beings who can walk about and touch things but cannot see. In time some of them develop the power of sight. All that they can tell their still blind friends about color would be unintelligible, and most importantly unverifiable. If this seeing group continued to discuss things that their blind friends could sense and understand, the communication would be trusting because the things under discussion would be verifiable. However, statments about color would remain unintelligible to the blind person. Thus, it would not be unreasonable for the blind person to believe that probably the seeing ones are able to perceive other aspects of reality and to describe correctly their statements about color although they remain unavailable and unintelligible to the blind persons.

The question at this point is whether it is reasonable to regard the agreement between the experiences of religious mystics as more like the agreement among trained microscopists about the detailed structure of cells, or as more like the agreement among habitual drunkards about the images of pink rats or snakes, or more like the agreement about colors which seeing persons would express in their statements to the blind men.

In case No. 2 society commonly believes that the habitual excessive use of alcoholic beverages is a cause of uniform delusion and not a source of additional information. The reason proposed by C. D. Broad is centered in the fact that the objects which drunkards claim to perceive are not fundamentally different in kind from the things sober people perceive.[53] We all see rats and snakes. Moreover, the drunkard claims that the rats and snakes which he sees are truly present in his room as much as his chairs and lamps are present. However, since these rats and snakes are the sort of thing we could see if we were there in the room, the fact that we cannot see them convinces us that they are not present. It therefore seems reasonable to conclude that the agreement among drunkards is a delusion and not a sign of special revelational experience.

In case No. 1 we feel fairly certain that the agreement among trained microscopists about the minute structure of cells expresses an objective fact although we cannot obtain similar experiences. We accept their special experiences as true because we understand the background of their activity. We know about the laws of optics, and about the skills that develop during the training of a scientist. As in other fields we learn to appreciate how trained people can detect things that untrained people will overlook.

In case No. 3 we consider another analogy to our understanding of religious experience. C. D. Broad54 remarks that many ideals of conduct and ways of life which we now recognize are good and useful, have been introduced by leaders who have had religious experiences. In this way we see the analogy to the case of the seeing man telling the men still blind about facts and objects that the blind men might one day verify for themselves. From these three cases C. D. Broad provides an opportunity for those of us who feel we have never had a religious experience to accept the possibility and likelihood of religious experiences in others. As long as there is a nucleus of agreement between the experiences of persons in different places, times and traditions demonstrating a tendency to put much the same interpretation in the cognitive content of these experiences, it is reasonable to interpret this agreement as a positive contact with objective aspects of reality. To think otherwise we must have a positive reason. C. D. Broad says:

> The practical postulate which we go upon everywhere else is to treat cognitive claims as veridical unless there be some positive reason to think them delusive. This after all is our only guarantee for believing that ordinary sense-perception is veridical. We cannot prove that what people agree upon in their perceiving really exists independently of them, but we do always assume that ordinary waking sense-perception is veridical unless we can produce some positive ground for thinking that it is delusive in any given case. I think it would be inconsistent to treat the experiences of religious mystics on different principles.55

During our childhood all of us were accustomed to accept the current common-sense and scientific views of the material world on the authority of our parents, teachers, and companions when we had neither the power nor the inclination to criticize these views. As we grew older the basic human tendency to believe in eye witnesses and to trust in authority figures remains. Our awareness of reality is always a shared awareness based on our mutual faith and trust.

Drugs and Religious Experience

Some years have passed since our attention focused on students of religion ingesting various drugs to determine their relation to religious experience. Theologians like A. R. Vidler[56] are now willing to accept R. C. Zachner's *Mysticism: Sacred and Profane* as having refuted the religious claims for mescalin. Yet Huston Smith[57] represents a group of scholars that believe it is time to reexamine the role of drugs in the history and phenomenology of religion.

Phenomenology pursues a careful description of human experience. How the experiences drugs induce differ from religious experiences is a particular challenge to the phenomenology of religion. Peter's Pentecostal experience shows that chemically induced psychic states can bear a resemblance to religious experience. Peter appealed to the criterion of time to defend those who were caught up in the Pentecostal experience against the charge of drunkenness. "These men are not drunk as you suppose, since it is only the third hour of the day" (Acts 2:15).

Huston Smith reminds us that there is no such thing as a drug experience *per se*, that is, no experience that the drugs alone provide.[58] Every experience is a mixture of three ingredients: the drug itself, the psychological make up of the individual, and the physical and social setting in which the drug is taken. Given the right combination of person and setting, Smith is convinced that drugs "can induce religious experiences indistinguishable from experiences that occur spontaneously."[59] He remarks further:

> The way the statistics are currently running, it looks as if from one-fourth to one-third of the general population will have religious experiences if they take the drugs under naturalistic conditions, meaning by this conditions in which the researcher supports the subject but does not try to influence the direction his experience will take. Among subjects who have strong religious inclinations to begin with, the proportion of those having religious experiences jump to three-fourths. If they take the drugs in settings that are religious too, the ratio soars to nine in ten.[60]

How does a phenomenologist determine that the experiences these people have are truly religious? Huston Smith begins with the fact that they say they are. He continues:

> The one-fourth to one-third of the general population figure is drawn from two sources. Ten months after they had their experiences, 24 per cent of the 194 subjects in a study by the California psychiatrist Oscar Janiger characterized their experiences as having been religious.[61] Thirty-two per cent of the 74 subjects in Ditman and Hayman's study reported, looking back on their LSD experience, that it looked as if it had been "very much" or "quite a bit" a religious experience; 42 per cent checked as true the statement that they "were left with a greater awareness of God, or a higher power, or ultimate reality."[63]

In the absence of any single definition of religious experience acceptable to the majority of psychologists of religion, Huston Smith believes there is no better way of telling whether the experiences of the persons involved in the above studies were religious than by stating whether they seemed religious to them.[63]

Walter Pahnke[64] applied a more rigorous method of determining if drug experiences can be religious. He administered psilocybin to ten theology students and professors in the setting of a Good Friday service. The drug was given "double blind," meaninig that neither Dr. Pahnke nor his subjects knew which ten were given psilocybin and which ten were given placebos to constitute a control group. The subsequent reports the subjects wrote of their experiences were placed successively before three college-graduate women who, without being informed about the nature of the study, were asked to rate each statement as to the degree (strong, moderate, slight, or none) to which the experience exemplified each of the nine traits of mystical experience enumerated in the typology of religious experience worked out in advance. The test showed that "those subjects who received psilocybin experienced phenomena which were indistinguishable from, if not identical with . . . the categories defined by our typology of mysticism."[65]

We must keep in mind that we are considering phenomenology and not ontology, description rather than interpretation. Why one person is more prone to religious experience than another is a separate question which we will not discuss at this time. If anything, the experiments show that drugs appear to be able to induce religious experiences. It is less evident that drugs produce religious lives. Consequently, we reaffirm our conviction that religion is more than religious experiences. The discussion about the role of drugs has many features helpful to the study of religious experience, but it also serves as a useful reminder that personal religious growth is more than the acquisition of desired states of religious experience and characteristics. The conclusion of Huston Smith is simply that "chemicals can aid the religious life, but only where set within a context of faith (meaning by this the conviction that what they disclose is true) and discipline (meaning diligent exercise of the will in the attempt to work out the implications of the disclosures for the living of life in the every-day, common sense world)."[66]

Summary

The foregoing phenomenological approach attempted to isolate and examine the chief aspects of religious experience so that its place can be understood in the overall investigation of religion.

Because any explanation of an experience is less than the experience itself, the usual study of religious experience amounts to a reflection about the event after the fact, but includes with it a desire to become more sensitive to the personal role of the subject of the religious experience.

Proceeding from Rudolf Otto's *Idea of the Holy*, philosophers and scientists of religion agree that the religious experience is both awesome and attractive. Consequently, there is a normal tendency to move the investigation of religious experience away from the concrete day to day living of the experiencer to a realm of reality shrouded in vagueness and mystery. However, by approaching the phenomena of religious experience realistically the student of religion avoids this tendency.

Revelation must be sharply distinguished from religious experience. Revelation is an unveiling of God's life and self according to Western believers. As such revelation supports religious life and growth for the total community. Religious experiences need not be revelation, i.e. revelatory for the total community. The religious experience may be limited entirely to the religious growth of one individual person who either works actively in a larger community or has little contact with a community of like believers.

Most of us will be content to find the object of our religion in the traditions of our own believing community. We will learn from the community our sense of the unifying principle or of God (depending on our religion), and we will let the leaders or prophets of the community set the tone for our living out of our personal religion. This manner of religion does not preclude religious experience as a possibility for most of us. Given the orientation of our culture various segments of our society will strive continually to be sensitive to the possibility of a personal religious experience to aid in the development of individual religiousness, and communal religiousness.

As the religious person admits his religious experiences, he moves to confirm them and allow them to enter his total being. These experiences continue to remain awesome and puzzling, but the subject begins to believe in them both as significant events in his personal life and as integral parts of reality. After a study of religious experiencers we see how a religious experience provides a basis for a global view of religious reality, but more importantly, we see how the religious experience as personal and individual carries with it the special power to touch deeply the life of the individual and the community in which he lives.

Discussion Questions

Chapter Six

1) Outline Panikkar's description of the three stages in which a person integrates himself into reality.

2) Discuss why any explanation of an experience is less than the experience itself.

3) Do you agree with Maslow that many people are capable of having "peak experiences" and in many cases these are religious experiences?

4) Discuss the characteristics of religious experience discovered by Kraft in his research. Are most of these characteristics acceptable to your idea of a religious experience?

5) Describe Kraft's idea of no-thingness related to holiness.

6) Compare the building block theory with the matrix theory of religious experience.

7) Discuss the differences between revelation and religious experience as Western theologians understand the terms.

8) Relate mystical experience to religious experience.

Notes

* Note the close relationship of Macquarrie's categories to those of Raimundo Panikkar at the beginning of this chapter.

1 Raimundo Panikkar, "The Ways of West and East," *New Dimensions in Religious Experience*, Proceedings of the College Theology Society, George Devine, editor (Staten Island: Alba House, 1971), p. 70.

2 *Ibid.*, p. 73.

3 Joachim Wach, *The Comparative Study of Religions* (New York: Columbia University Press, 1958), p. 30.

4 *Ibid.*, p. 38.

5 *Ibid.*, p. 38 citing R.R. Marett in *Sacraments of Simple Folk* (Oxford: Clarendon Press, 1953), p. 3.

6 *Ibid.*, p. 40.

7 *Ibid.*, p. 40.

8 *Ibid.*, p. 44 citing William Temple, *Nature, Man and God* (Gifford Lectures, 1932-34) (New York: Macmillan Co., 1949), p. 306ff.

9 *Ibid.*, p. 46.

10 *Ibid.*, p. 46.

11 *Ibid.*, p. 48, citing Lewis Richard Farness, *Attributes of God* (Oxford: Clarendon Press, 1925), p. 11.

12 *Ibid.*, p. 49.

13 *Ibid.*, p. 54 citing Mircea Eliade, *Traite d'histoire des religions* (Paris: Payot, 1949), p. 16.

14 Abraham H. Maslow, *Religions, Values and Peak-Experiences* (New York: The Viking Press, 1964), p. 23.

15 *Ibid.*, p. 32.

16 Abraham H. Maslow, *Toward a Psychology of Being* (New York: D. Van Norstrand Co., 1968), p. 71.

17 Maslow, *Religions, Values and Peak-Experiences, op. cit.*, p. 59ff.

18 William Kraft, *The Search for The Holy* (Philadelphia: The Westminster Press, 1971), p. 25.

19 *Ibid.*, p. 25.

20 *Ibid.*, p. 39.

21 *Ibid.*, p. 40.

22 *Ibid.*, p. 44.

23 *Ibid.*, p. 44.

24 *Ibid.*, p. 52.

25 *Ibid.*, p. 72.

26 *Ibid.*, p. 75.

27 *Ibid.*, p. 76.

28 *Ibid.*, p. 78.

29 *Ibid.*, p. 79.

30 *Ibid.*, p. 82ff.

31 Rem B. Edwards, *Reason and Religion* (New York: Harcourt, Brace, Jovanovich, Inc., 1972), pp. 299-301.

32 *Ibid.*, p. 293.

33 *Ibid.*, p. 295.

34 *Ibid.*, p. 296.

35 *Ibid.*, p. 297.

36 *Ibid.*, p. 297.

37 *Ibid.*, p. 298.

38 *Ibid.*, pp. 299-300.

39 C. D. Broad, "The Appeal to Religious Experience," *Philosophy of Religion*, William L. Rowe and William J. Wainwright (editors), (New York: Harcourt, Brace, Jovanovich, Inc., 1973), p. 310.

40 John Macquarrie, *Principles of Christian Theology* (New York: Charles Scribner's Sons, 1966), p. 75ff.

41 *Ibid.*, p. 7.

42 *Ibid.*, p. 84.

43 *Ibid.*, p. 85.

44 *Ibid.*, p. 86.

45 Walter Stace, "Subjectivity, Objectivity and the Self," *Philosophy of Religion*, William L. Rowe and William J. Wainwright (editors), (New York: Harcourt, Brace, Jovanovich, Inc., 1973), pp. 276-77.

46 *Ibid.*, p. 276.

47 *Ibid.*, pp. 276-77.

48 *Ibid.*, p. 268.

49 *Ibid.*, p. 269.

50 *Ibid.*, p. 271.

51 *Ibid.*, pp. 269-70.

52 C. D. Broad, *op. cit.*, pp. 311ff.

53 *Ibid.*, p. 312.

54 *Ibid.*, p. 313.

55 *Ibid.*, pp. 313-14.

56 Cf. footnote listing essays in *Soundings* in Huston Smith, "Do Drugs Have Religious Import," *Philosophy of Religion*, William L. Rowe and William J. Wainwright (editors), (New York: Harcourt, Brace, Jovanovich, Inc., 1973), p. 326.

57 *Ibid.*, p. 326.

58 *Ibid.*, p. 328.

59 *Ibid.*, p. 328.

60 *Ibid.*, p. 328.

61 *Ibid.*, Cf. listing under footnote No. 9, p. 328.

62 *Ibid.*, Cf. listing under footnote No. 10, p. 328.

63 *Ibid.*, p. 329.

64 *Ibid.*, p. 329.

65 *Ibid.*, p. 329 in which the author quotes from: "Drugs and Mysticism: An Analysis of the Relationship between Psychedelic Drugs and the Mystical

Consciousness," a thesis presented to the Committee on Higher Degrees in History and Philosophy of Religion, Harvard University, June 1983.

66 *Ibid.*, p. 336.

Chapter Seven

Personal Choices

Looking at the modern world of religion through the eyes of sociology, Peter Berger[1] alerts us to the multiple choices available to us in the technological world. Admitting to various forces that shape our modern attitudes both externally and internally, we accept these forces as active within the realm of free choice. By contrast, premodern persons lived in what was for the most part a world of fate. Their tools, clothing, conveyance, and livelihood were, for them, all limited choices. Where formerly there were one or two choices, now there are hundreds. And when we think of our world and of the possible values and ways of regarding this world today we say with Peter Berger: "Modernity pluralizes."[2] With that in mind, today more than ever, persons require social confirmation for their beliefs about reality, especially religious or philosophical reality.

With multiple choices, more ideas and values become plausible. To a sociologist, society lends support to these ideas by providing plausibility structures capable of confirming beliefs about reality. Thus, it is that this relationship between a society and individual consciousness lends support to multiple plausibility structures. As society becomes more complex, more choices are available − with or without society's support. Indeed, because of its complexity and pluriformity modern society will tend to be less reliable[3] in lending support to specific individual values and ideas than society in the past. Yet modern man should see his choices as a gift. In sharp contrast to the former world inhabited by traditional man, modern man must make choices in the area of beliefs, values, and world views. Making these choices requires reflection. Whereby premodern persons would act spontaneously, modern persons must reflect and engage in more deliberate thought.

Moving from fate in premodern times to choice today with its built-in pluralism, we live out an uneasy freedom. Religion today requires each person to accept the burden of choosing his or her own religious value system.

The verb, to choose, from the Greek, is *hairein*. The modern work "heresy" comes from this verb. *Hairesis* originally meant the "taking" of a choice. Derived from that is the idea of taking an opinion. Eventually, according to religious language, one who made a choice outside the usual authority structure was considered a heretic. Today in our fast-paced world, all of us who ultimately seize a religious denomination or sect make a choice because we are free to choose. This action represents the modern expression of heresy. For premodern persons, heresy was a remote possibility, for modern person, heresy typically becomes a necessity.[4]

Berger develops this idea of choice in his book, *The Heretical Imperative*. Modern times demand we make choices, in religion as elsewhere. Our dignity and destiny are wrapped in this pluralistic milieu. We cannot avoid these choices without inflicting pain and hurt on our own personality. The question is: what choices can we make in religion today? For Berger, three basic options present themselves for religious thought within a pluralistic situation. He calls them the deductive, reductive, and inductive options.[5]

The Three Options

The deductive option reasserts the authority of a religious tradition in the face of modern secularity. The reductive option reinterprets the tradition in terms of the modern world. In this way the authority of modern thought or consciousness is substituted for the authority of the tradition.

The inductive option turns to experience as the ground for all religious affirmations. One's own experience, to whatever extent that is possible, and the experience embodied in a particular range of traditions are compared. Avoiding specific authority, this third option is preferred by Berger because of its open-mindedness both to tradition and to one's own experience in relation to the tradition. Inspired by the theological liberalism of Friederich Schleiermacher Berger turns from authority to experience as a focus for religious thought and living. This third option provides both stability and flexibility for assessing religion in a modern pluralistic world. Let us compare these options in greater detail.

The Deductive Option

The first option reaffirms tradition. As such it is often called neo-orthodoxy or dialectical theology. Karl Barth led this movement that spanned the two Great Wars in Europe. Barth and his followers centered attention on the God of Christians who speaks to mankind in revelation. The word of God coming to us from the prophets and later on through the Scriptures, according to Barth, is made alive in the current preaching of the church. The word of God is given to the Christian believer. It precedes all reflection on our part, but calls for our response, a response that presupposes faith. Theology for Barth engages the believer as both an intellectual activity and as a prolonged act of faith. Such faith is a result of God's grace. The human person can know nothing about God except what God has revealed about himself. To the neo-orthodox person, faith is presupposed. The issue is: How do we respond in faith to God's revelation? For neo-orthodoxy a person does not have an innate capacity to experience the divine; only the Word itself gives the capacity to affirm the Word of God.

Where does experience fit into neo-orthodoxy? Religious experience as the starting point of theological reflection is clearly rejected. Experience of God's Word is possible, but only by means of God's Word. Every human response to the Word is exclusively determined by God's Grace.[6] Thus the experience of God's Word cannot be rooted in any anthropologically given condition. The experience of God is brought about only by faith.

The problem in neo-orthodoxy is faith. Until one has faith, one cannot have an experience of God, nor (more critical to our question), can one experience religion. Kierkegaard recommends that the individual may confront the message embodied in the tradition and by a wrenching existential effort leap into the position of saying: "Yes, I believe." Kierkegaard, according to Berger, is the specter that haunts the Barthian statement.[7]

Neo-orthodoxy constantly confronts the problem whether or not Christianity is the true religion. For the neo-orthodox person any faith is always Christian; any religion is always Christian. But the modern world asks: Where should I leap in faith? How do I know that among all the choices I will arrive in the Christian act of faith? Neo-orthodoxy denies the multiplicity of traditions or authorities, but Christianity is one religion among many.   Neo-orthodoxy wishes to cut across these varieties and deny the reality of pluralism.   In view of this denial, the individual is not consoled as he seeks to identify his religious experiences.

The Reductive Approach — Modernizing Tradition

Each of us is put into a world not of our own making. This "situatedness" compels us to reflect on issues not only in themselves but also as they affect us now in our world. Today the "gods" of religion seem to have receded from the main stream of society. While neo-orthodox minds may deny our present situation, the modern reductive possibility confronts our present world and attempts to place religion with some relevance into this present situation.

Berger[8] notes that the modern situation brings about an adversary relationship between a social secularity and personal religious consciousness. This relationship creates cognitive pressure for the individual ultimately resulting in cognitive bargaining between the past traditions and present secularity, between old religious views and modern modifications of these views. For example, the miracle of the loaves and fishes may now be explained in naturalistic terms, but the miracle of Christ's resurrection remains intact. Bultmann's process of demythologizing the Scriptures in the contemporary secularized world after 1945 created a reflective process that confronted orthodoxy directly and urged Christianity to update itself lest the mythological description of God, man, the heavens and the earth, fade into oblivion.

Modern man can reflect in religious and mythological terms but he is bound to the view of the world that science has given him. For followers of Bultmann Christianity must move beyond cognitive bargaining to demythologize the entire Christian message called the kerygma. The heart of the Christian message or kerygma must be maintained, but it must be communicated to modern man in a nonmythological form.[9] The issue for the Christian is not the history of the Risen Christ, but the history and reflection of those who believed in the Risen Christ. The Easter faith of the primitive Christian community becomes critical. Also, how this faith relates to modern persons is important. In this reductive view the Christian life today must live out a secularized faith that acknowledges a transcendent God and a continuing, ever growing tradition.

The main difficulty of the reductive option is the inability of religious people to stop the secularization process. Eventually this modern concept could become self-liquidating. Bultmann as symbolic leader of this option might call for a demythologization that falsely extolls the present intellectual powers of modern man. Is it not possible that while gaining some important insights into reality, modern man has also lost some equally valid insights. Technically, the secularizing of theology runs the risk of developing an improper perspective of a specific religious tradition. Simply because we have computers and space travel experience, we do not have reason to dismiss all of the transcendent ideas of God coming from the past. Indeed, we cannot update religion simply by dismissing all of the previous primitive views about it.

By analogy when we hear of a traveler returning home from some faraway land we can assume tht his account of his trip will reflect the past history of his life, the social problems he has suffered, and the economic conditions surrounding his home life from a very tender age. Consequently it is plausible for the traveler to perceive the faraway country as a giant projection of his own country. Indeed, the traveler's account will be useful in gaining a better understanding of our own country. None of his account however invalidates the proposition that the faraway country does exist and something about it can be learned from the traveler. The issue is not that Marco Polo was Italian and consequently spoke with all sorts of class resentments, anxieties, and unresolved complexes. The issue rather is – Marco Polo did visit China and lived to tell about it.

Our ancestors' views about God and religion may have been limited by their experiences, complexes, and myths, but nonetheless they had religious experiences and we must come to grips with this fact. The reductive possibility indeed constantly updates, but without being always clearly aware that each age transcends the bounds of its prior age to describe its own religious sense.

Inductive Possibility

Using the term induction in its most common sense, that is, arguing from empirical evidence, Berger consider this third possibility as the most reasonable one for religion today. Under this system, the individual takes his own human experience of religion as a starting point. He compares the experience as it grows and evolves with the experience that the historian is able to uncover in the various religious traditions. Liberal Protestants under the paradigmatic figure of Friedrich Schleiermacher have used the method at least for the past century, and perhaps in some limited form, before the 19th century.

Reared in Pietist schools, Schleiermacher emphasized personal religious experience as the focus of religious activity. The Romantic movement used the word feeling (Gefühl) almost in the same way Schleiermacher uses experience. For Schleiermacher the human experience of faith involves the total person, but this experience is registered externally as feeling, i.e. a consciousness (inductively examined) of one's contact with the center of the Universe.

Rather than beginning with revelation, outside the person, an inquirer in Schleiermacher's system begins with his own experience of religion. As he reflects upon this experience he opens himself up to a sense of dependence and to a relationship to the infinite. Schleiermacher begs us to let him speak of a personal view of religion. He begins by describing the endearing piety that originates in our mother's womb.[10] There piety grows and later, as family life develops, it shows itself in humility. The faith of our fathers is sifted and cleansed from the rubbish of antiquity. It seems to Schleiermacher that in our youthful doubts God and immortality vanish, but in reality, God remains in me — unnoticed.

As we grow we learn friendship and love. We cling to holiness, wholeness, and piety. Eventually, we talk of religion only because we live religion in our personal reflection. Schleiermacher like Whitehead believes we learn of religion nowhere else but in the interior of our personal existence. The religion we find in the sacred books is not compelling. Schleiermacher says: "To the man who has not himself experienced it, it would only be an annoyance and a folly."[11] Thus, Schleiermacher asks us to find the heart of religion by looking inward to our emotions and dispositions as if in juxtaposition with the acts and utterances of inspired men in history.

The Nature of Religion

Religion is not accustomed to appear openly, but is only seen in secret by those who love it.[12] Religion is as complex as man himself who contemplates it. At one time it is a way of thinking, a peculiar way of contemplating the world. At another it is a way of acting, a special desire, and love. Religion as both science and art strives always for piety in a contemplative manner. Schleiermacher explains:

> The contemplation of the pious is the immediate consciousness of the universal existence of all finite things, in and through the infinite, and of all temporal things in and through the eternal.[13]

Using knowledge and science as springboards, religion for
Schleiermacher is an affection, a revelation of the Infinite in the finite. For a Westerner this Infinite Being is called God.

It is with the understanding of piety that we are able to pene-
trate into Schleiermacher's idea of dependence and liberty. In *The
Christian Faith* he says: "The common element in all howsoever diverse expressions of piety by which these are distinguished from all
other feelings, or, in other words, the self identical essence of piety
is this; the consciousness of being absolutely dependent, or, which
is the same thing, of being in relation with God."[14] Religious piety
is basically a person's relationship with God understood as self consciousness.   In self-consciousness Schleiermacher lists two elements:

1)   one expresses the existence of the subject for itself
2)   the other expresses its coexistence with an Other.[15]

The common element in all determinations of self consciousness
that predominantly expresses a receptivity from the outside is the
feeling of dependence. On the other hand, he reminds us that the
common element in all these determinations that predominantly
expresses spontaneous movement and activity is the feeling of
freedom. Schleiermacher considers the feeling of dependence and
the feeling of freedom as one.[16] He uses the examples of children
and private citizens who express at times one feeling more sharply
than the other, but nonetheless both feelings exist in the unity of
the person in our own world of experience. The sense of feeling
dependent joined to the sense of being free is a person's basic relationship that includes all other relationships in it.

The man of this world who only thinks methodically and who
acts from personal principle and design, and wants to accomplish
this or that goal in the world unavoidably circumscribes himself,
and makes everything that does not forward his goals an object of
antipathy. When, however, the free impulse of seeing and of living
is directed towards the Infinite and goes into the Infinite the mind
is released in unbounded liberty.   Religion alone according to

Schleiermacher[17] rescues us from the heavy fetters of opinion and desire. As an act of freedom and as a feeling religion encompasses two elements:

1) the individual surrenders himself to the Universe and is influenced by that side turned towards him. (An apt phrase might be: Bloom where you are planted.)

2) he takes this feeling and contact and brings it into the inner unity of his life and being.

The amazing impact of these two elements cuts us to the core of our integrity and humility. Most of us will not cooperate with the process because of its overwhelming implications. A person who enacts these two elements becomes a religious person, but alas, how vulnerable, how open to disappointment by the threatening measures of the world that insists: "Be or do . . . this way!"

Almost as if being caught up in the classic line of Hollywood comedy, "Walk this way," only to proceed to follow the butler, or waiter with the same halting manner or gait he demonstrates, religion more than anything else calls for leadership in our lives when most of all we desire from religion only that we be followers. If religion calls us to be leaders, what about the element of fear?

Fear

Fear is not a part of religion, yet much of our historical experience of the Christian religion is based on fear. The infinite, if we reflect upon it for any length of time is threatening, but does not the infinite also show a humility? Do we find the infinite interfering in our life, dictating responses of life's questions? No. But as we grow in piety we slowly appreciate, respect, and eventually love the infinite. The joy of religion is a sense of the love one has for the infinite.

The sense of the Whole must be found first in our own minds[18] and from there it must be transferred to corporeal nature. The total universe portrays itself in the inner life. Thence the corporeal is comprehensible from the spiritual.

Religion and Humanity

Religion and humanity in this inductive model are closely united. In order to receive the life of the world-spirit and have religion, each of us must first in love and through love have found humanity.[19] A longing for love, ever satisfied, ever again renewed, forthwith becomes religion.

Since each person embraces most warmly the person in whom the world mirrors itself for him or her, most clearly and purely, he is given the chance to move from the love of man to the love of God. Schleiermacher laments the excessive stress of mankind on man. He sees us as idealists taking persons individually and desiring each to show a fullness of dignity. Yet, no one person corresponds to this ideal. To solve this problem, Schleiermacher recommends that we look at undivided humanity. He says: "Work on individuals but rise in contemplation, on the wings of religion, to endless undivided humanity. Seek this humanity in each individual, regard the nature of every person as one revelation of it."[20] With this advice we refrain from overemphasizing the requirements for human living. Rather we let the ideal of religion be the absorbing factor and regard individual persons as our anthropological starting point and only a starting point for contemplation of the infinite. Schleiermacher constantly compares the world, mankind, and God in related patterns that shed light on our religious nature. His thoughts tease us to attention until we begin to reflect upon the basic unity we all seek in the reality around us.[21]

Awareness

How do you and I feel about our relation to the continuing current of the world? Religion draws us out of mere self-will into this current and challenges us to recognize the dignity and worth of this type of dependence. As we gradually sense the path of humanity and of our relation to it, the whole becomes clearer to us and we are freed from our dependence on our own fleeting being. We see how we fit in this world. We advance humbly but serenely in a posture of freedom. The passage through these different feelings is the experience of religion. This experience of humanity is indeed for Schleiermacher the experience of religion.[22] For him religion is the sum of all higher feelings. As a resolution for any lingering of blind instinct, unthinking custom, dull obedience, attitudes lazy and passive, all symptoms of freedom forsaken and humanity neutralized, religion binds us to nature and identifies the highest feelings of this bond.

The Exercise of Religious Feelings

What is essential to religion? For Schleiermacher very little outside of contemplating the infinite is considered essential. Schleiermacher compares our conceptions from experience to the conceptions of a religious person. Eventually from religious conceptions come doctrines and dogmas. Piety reflected in miracle, revelation, and inspiration all show openness to sharing and comparing what is essentially religious in one's experience. But we apply science to estimate precisely what a miracle is, or in what revelation consists. Religion is confused, if the inquirer fails to allow physics and allied sciences to stand by themselves as tools for investigation. In religion every finite person, thing, and event is a sign of the infinite. A miracle is simply the religious name for event. Every event according to Schleiermacher becomes a miracle as soon as the religious aspect of it can become the dominant aspect.[23] Thus the more religious one is, the more miracles one acknowledges.

The religious person has to sense his religion in freedom. His belief is always based on a personal understanding of religion. Belief in another's religion, or simply in sacred writing is not religion. Rather, a lively and immediate understanding of the writing and of his freedom to do without it characterizes the religious person.[24]

For Schleiermacher God the infinite is the source of all our feelings and understanding of religion. Any feeling or emotion of piety has value only insofar as it comes as a revelation of God. To see the world as a Whole is done only in God. Thus, typical emotions produced by the world's events are distinguished from a feeling of God, an immediate (as opposed to mediated) consciousness of the Deity as is found in ourselves and in the world.

The inductive method ties itself to two important operations in the scientific study of religion: the historical operation and the phenomenological operation. These two operations precede an assessment of revelation which Schleiermacher considers as "every original and new disclosure of the universe and its innermost life to man."[25] For Schleiermacher various revelations were possible. He was not committed to one specific revelation. In the inductive method inspired by Schleiermacher every religion is traced back to its experiential source. To choose a certain source, is to highlight it among all other. This choice, in effect, is a heresy, one, Berger, might add, is necessary for every religious person.

Midst all religious traditions, Schleiermacher chooses Christianity as the ideal religion. He considers Christ as mediator, the one who most perfectly expresses the infinite in the finite. The christocentric aspect of Schleiermacher's theology allows for a healthy view of the process of secularizing Christianity, but the inductive approach further demands each person to compare his own experience of religion with the tradition he wishes to examine and absorb. The reductive approach, however, does not require this comparison.

To Schleiermacher the heart of a specifically Christian religious experience is consequently an awareness of Christ as mediator between God and man. The Scriptures are used to give testimony or witness to this experience. The Scriptures grew out of their own strength and amicably would allow other writings to join them if the community saw them as having the same strength.

In the inductive model experience is prior to any theories or doctrines about it. Christ as leader of the Christian tradition is compared with our own consciousness of our religious experience. In this way, the orthodoxy of Christianity remains intact, but it is examined in the light of human experience which grows and reflects upon its relation to the Infinite. This examination as the ongoing quest for the essence of Christianity is able to be known by an individual believer at any given time in history.

Critique of the Inductive Model

Schleiermacher and his followers, Albrecht Ritschl and Adolf Von Harnack, admitted to the tendency to reduce Christianity to our present historical impression of it, but they studiously avoided this tendency. Mere updating of Christianity to show its present cultural and ethical merit is not the proper exercise of the Inductive model. More is required.

In the Inductive model one reflects on one's own faith, and view of religion. This amounts to a gathering of data or evidence about religious experience. Thus faith and inductive reasoning stand in dialectical relationship to each other. First I consider that I believe and then I reflect on what this means. I gather evidence − available to me − about that which is the object of my faith. This evidence is rooted in my present experience, past experience, and my experience of the traditions of my belief handed down through the centuries.

This method does not reduce theology to anthropology as Feuerbach recommends, but starts with and builds upon the anthropological given − experience. Obviously, there are weaknesses built into this system because I must estimate my starting point before I move on to more objective analysis of the traditions. This inductive model admits this risk, but demands nevertheless we continue the process.

Even if we fail in the use of this method we record in some limited way our sense of religion, the contemporary world view of our chief religious traditions, and the historical perspective of these traditions. For Berger it is the historical discipline[26] which more than any other instrument is able to retrieve the immediacy of religion out of the dying embers of tradition.

How am I to identify my religious experience? Peter Berger reviews the list of experts on the subject only to conclude that the only way to distinguish "true" from "false" religious experience is to weigh the insight purported to come from the experience on the practical scale of reason. The inquirer asks: in view of all other empirical experiences of religion, and in respect for my knowledge of my human condition, how do I assess this experience that readily could be called religious?

The inductive model, like the two preceding models, would like to arrive at religious certitude once the process is complete. But, alas, the nature of religion, religious experience, and the limits of the inquirer knowing anything, demand an humble posture in accepting religion inductively by means of this model. Religious searching requires truth, but not in the sense of absolute truth. The certitude attainable on this earth of any knowable material depends directly on the complexity and availability of knowledge concerning the material. It is easier to learn the quantity or dimensions of a land mass than it is to determine the culture of its inhabitants. Religion of its very nature sets limits on us. The inductive model in all its phases must accept this problem.

Conclusions

As noted by Peter Berger and other religious thinkers today, Schleiermacher prompts us to see the individual as the starting point for religion. If we add Whitehead and James to the group there is a strong support for Schleiermacher's inductive approach. The complexity of the world allows us to fall so readily into a "group-think" approach to religion. After all, the community is our usual support, be it family or nation. The question again looms high over other religious questions. How am I a religious person? Is religion more an individual or communal matter in my life?

I see religion as expressed in America today to be a thread passed back and forth between the two poles of individuality and community. The constant weaving back and forth creates a series of lines, eventually a fabric that incorporates in the person that freedom to search individually for an authentic understanding of religious life and faith while meeting the community with all its traditions and attitudes, ready to advise, cajole, or even persuade the individual to accept a certain common view of religion.

The two poles, individual and communal, support the weave of life, religious life. Requirements of being tied to each pole in some harmonious and balanced threading process is desirable. We are all too social to give up our forebears and our neighbors, but since the age of Marx and Engels we value our freedom to think and to act as individuals. Because freedom is so new to our Western culture we must still struggle to learn what it means to be free individuals seeking the wisdom and understanding of all that is valuable in the larger community.

This brief study calls for a caution rather than a conclusion. The poles remain. Individual and communal both have a position of dignity in our personal life. We cannot risk rugged individualism to the neglect of communal response. We cannot yield to the larger community and give up our rights of religious citizenship. We flounder in order to flourish, we become sidetracked, confused, only because it is the human way to grow and to move forward.

Today fate yields to choice, and in our struggle with this uneasy freedom we enjoy, we move from authority to experience as our personal focus for religious living. At Schleiermacher's bidding we look to individuals, and as we review our religious values, we rise in contemplation to endless undivided humanity. We refrain from overemphasizing the requirements for human living, but see religion as an anthropological starting point for the full contemplation of the infinite.

Discussion Questions

Chapter Seven

1) Do you agree with Peter Berger when he contends that we must all be heretics today?

2) Outline and discuss the three options Berger makes available for religious choice today.

3) Explain Schleiermacher's approach to religion including the advantages and disadvantages of his approach.

4) Why does Schleiermacher consider Christianity as the ideal religion?

Notes

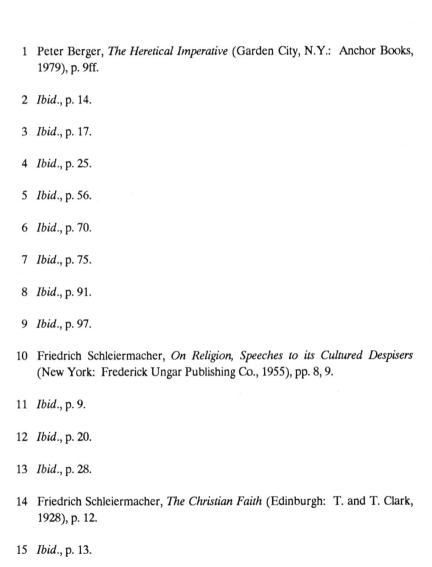

1 Peter Berger, *The Heretical Imperative* (Garden City, N.Y.: Anchor Books, 1979), p. 9ff.

2 *Ibid.*, p. 14.

3 *Ibid.*, p. 17.

4 *Ibid.*, p. 25.

5 *Ibid.*, p. 56.

6 *Ibid.*, p. 70.

7 *Ibid.*, p. 75.

8 *Ibid.*, p. 91.

9 *Ibid.*, p. 97.

10 Friedrich Schleiermacher, *On Religion, Speeches to its Cultured Despisers* (New York: Frederick Ungar Publishing Co., 1955), pp. 8, 9.

11 *Ibid.*, p. 9.

12 *Ibid.*, p. 20.

13 *Ibid.*, p. 28.

14 Friedrich Schleiermacher, *The Christian Faith* (Edinburgh: T. and T. Clark, 1928), p. 12.

15 *Ibid.*, p. 13.

16 *Ibid.*, pp. 14, 15.

17 Friedrich Schleiermacher, *On Religion, op. cit.*, p. 46.

18 *Ibid.*, p. 58.

19 *Ibid.*, p. 59.

20 *Ibid.*, p. 60.

21 *Ibid.*, p. 62.

22 *Ibid.*, pp. 65, 66.

23 *Ibid.*, p. 73.

24 *Ibid.*, p. 75.

25 Peter Berger, *op. cit.*, p. 119 in which Berger quotes Schleiermacher in *Uber Die Religion in Samliche Werke* I (Berlin: Reinyer, 1843), p. 249.

26 *Ibid.*, pp. 131, 132

A Beginner's Reading List in Religion

Sociology of Religion

Max Weber, *The Sociology of Religion.* Boston: Beacon Press, 1933.

Peter L. Berger, *The Sacred Canopy.* New York: Doubleday and Co., Inc., 1967.

Emile Durkheim, *The Elementary Forms of the Religious Life* (trans. by Swain). London: Collier Books, 1961.

Robert N. Bellah, *Beyond Belief.* New York: Harper and Row, Publishers, 1970.

Phenomenology of Religion

G. Van der Leeuw, *Religion in Essence and Manifestation* (2 vols.). New York: Harper & Row, 1963.

Mircea Eliade, *Patterns in Comparative Religion.* New York: The World Publishing Co., 1958.

Mircea Eliade, *The Sacred and the Profane.* New York: Harcourt, Brace & World, Inc., 1959.

Joachim Wach, *The Comparative Study of Religions.* New York: Columbia University Press, 1958.

Rudolf Otto, *The Idea of the Holy.* London: Oxford University Press, 1923.

Psychology of Religion

William James, *The Varieties of Religious Experience*. New York: Mentor Books, 1958.

Gordon Allport, *The Individual and his Religion*. New York: The Macmillan Co., 1950.

Christian Religion and Religions (Compared):

A) *Doctrines*

Paul Tillich, *Dynamics of Faith*. New York: Harper & Row, 1957.

John Macquarrie, *Principles of Christian Theology*. New York: Charles Scribner's Sons, 1966.

B) *History*

Huston Smith, *The Religions of Man*. New York: Harper & Row, 1958.

David Bradley, *A Guide to the World's Religions*. Englewood Cliffs, N.J.: Prentice Hall Inc., 1963.

Philosophy of Religion:

Rem B. Edwards, *Reason and Religion*. New York: Harcourt, Brace, Jovanovich, Inc., 1972.

Norbert O. Schedler, *Philosophy of Religion*. New York: Macmillan Publishing Co., 1974.

Selected Bibliography

Allport, Gordon W. *The Individual and His Religion*. New York: The Macmillan Company, 1950.

Allport, Vernon, Lindzay. *Study of Values*. New York: Houghton-Mifflin, 1962.

Argyle, Michael, Ben Samin Beit-Hallahmi. *The Social Psychology of Religion*. London: Routledge & Kegan Paul Ltd., 1975.

Barbour, Ian G. "Teilhard's Process Metaphysics," *Process Theology*. Ewert H. Cousins, editor. New York: Newman Press, 1971.

Barbour, Ian. *Issues in Science and Religion*. Englewood Cliffs, New Jersey: Prentice Hall, 1966.

Bellah, Robert N. "The Role of Preaching in a Corrupt Republic," *Christianity Crisis*, December 25, 1978, pp. 317-22.

Bellah, Robert N. "Religion in the University," *Religion in the Undergraduate Curriculum: An Analysis and Interpretation*. Washington, D.C.: Association of American Colleges, 1972.

Bellah, Robert N. "Christian Realism," *Theology Today*, Volume XXVI, January, 1970, No. 4.

Bellah, Robert. *Beyond Belief*. New York: Harper and Row Publishers, 1970.

Berger, Peter L. *The Social Reality of Religion*. London: Faber and Faber, 1967.

Berger, Peter L. *The Heretical Imperative*. Garden City, N.Y.: Anchor Press/Doubleday, 1979.

Berger, Peter L. *Rumor of Angels*. Garden City, N.Y.: Doubleday, 1969.

Berger, Peter L. *Sacred Canopy*. Garden City, N.Y.: Doubleday, 1967.

Bergson, Henri. *The Two Sources of Religion and Morality*. New York: H. Holt and Company, 1935.

Bidney, David. *Theoretical Anthropology*. New York: Columbia University Press, 1953.

Bradley, David G. *A Guide to the World's Religions*. Englewood Cliffs, N.J.: Prentice Hall, Inc.

Broad, C. D. "The Appeal to Religious Experience," *Philosophy of Religion*. William L. Rowe and William J. Wainwright, editors. New York: Harcourt, Brace, Jovanovich, Inc., 1973.

Bultmann, Rudolf Karl. *Kerygma and Myth: A Theological Debate*. Ed. Hans Werner Bartsch. New York: Harper and Row, Publishers, 1961.

Caillois, Roger. *Man and the Sacred*. Glencoe, Ill.: The Free Press, 1959.

Calinesco, Matei. "Imagination and Meaning: Aesthetic Attitudes and Ideas in Mircea Eliade's Thought," *Journal of Religion*, January, 1977, pp. 1-15.

Christianity and Crisis, September 17, 1973.

Clark, Walter Houson. *The Psychology of Religion*. New York: The Macmillan Co., 1958.

Cobb, John B. "The World and God," *Process Theology*. Ewert H. Cousins, editor. New York: Newman Press, 1971.

Comstock, W. Richard. "Toward Open Definitions of Religion," *Journal of the American Academy of Religion*, LII (September, 1984), 499-517.

Cousins, Ewert H. "Process Models in Culture, Philosophy, and Theology," *Process Theology*. Ewert H. Cousins, editor. New York: Newman Press, 1971, pp. 7, 8.

Deats, Paul K., Jr., ed. *Towards a Discipline of Social Ethics*. Boston: Boston University Press, 1972.

Douglas, Jack D. *The Relevance of Sociology*. New York: Appleton-Century-Crofts, 1970.

Durkheim, Emile. *Elementary Forms of the Religious Life*. Glencoe, Ill.: Free Press, 1947.

Edward, David Lawrence. *Religion and Change*. New York: Harper and Row Publishers, 1969.

Edwards, Rem B. *Reason and Religion*. New York: Harcourt, Brace, Jovanovich, Inc., 1972.

Eister, Allan W., editor. *Changing Perspectives in the Scientific Study of Religion*. New York: John Wiley & Sons, 1974.

Eister, Allan W. "Religion and Science, A.D. 1977," *Journal for the Scientific Study of Religion*, December, 1978, pp. 347-58.

Eliade, Mircea and Joseph M. Kitagawa, eds. *The History of Religions: Essays in Methodology*. Chicago and London: University of Chicago Press, 1959.

Eliade, Mircea. *The Quest*. Chicago: The University of Chicago Press, 1959.

Eliade, Mircea. *Patterns of Comparative Religion*. New York: Meridian Books, The World Publishing Co., 1958.

Eliade, Mircea. *The Forge and the Crucibles*. London: Rider & Co., 1962.

Eliade, Mircea. *Traite d'Histoire des Religions*. Paris: Payot, 1949.

Eliade, Mircea. *Myth and Reality*. New York: Harper and Row, Publishers, 1963.

Ellul, Jacques. *The New Demons*. London: Mowbrays, 1975.

Ellwood, Robert S., Jr. *Introducing Religion from Inside and Outside*. Englewood Cliffs, N.J.: Prentice Hall, Inc., 1978.

Fallding, Harold. *The Sociology of Religion*. London: McGraw-Hill Ryerson Ltd., 1974.

Farness, Lewis Richard. *Attributes of God*. Oxford: Clarendon Press, 1925.

Feuerbach, Ludwig Andreas. *The Essence of Faith According to Luther*. Ed. Melvin Cherno. New York: Harper, 1967.

Finney, John M. "Fichter's Concept of Man in Social Science: A Comment," *J.S.S.R.*, Vol. 12, No. 1, March 1973.

Fontinell, Eugene. *Towards a Reconstruction of Religion*. Garden City, N.Y.: Doubleday & Co., 1970.

Fowler, Dean R. "Alfred North Whitehead," *Zygon*, XI, 1 (March, 1976): 50-69.

Geertz, Clifford. "Religion as a Cultural System," *Anthropological Approaches to the Study of Religion*, Michael Banton, Ed. A.S.A. Monographs, vol. 3. London: Fairstock Press, 1966.

Glock, Charles Y. and Rodney Stark. *Religion and Society in Tension*. Chicago: Rand McNally Press, 1965.

Grensted, L.W. *The Psychology of Religion*. London: Oxford University Press, 1952.

Hageman, Alice. "Liberating Theology through Action." *The Christian Century*, October 1, 1975, pp. 850-53.

Hartshorne, Charles. "The Development of Process Philosophy," *Process Theology*. Ewert H. Cousins, editor. New York: Newman Press, 1971.

Hartshorne, Charles. "Philosophical and Religious Uses of God," *Process Theology*. Ewert H. Cousins, editor. New York: Newman Press, 1971.

Hartshorne, Charles. *A Natural Theology for Our Time*. La Salle, Ill.: Open Court Publishing Co., 1967.

Hartshorne, Charles. *Creative Synthesis and Philosophic Method*. La Salle, Ill.: Open Court Publishing Co., 1970.

Henry, Carl F. H., ed. *Revelation and the Bible: Contemporary Evangelical Thought*. Grand Rapids: Baker Book House, 1958.

Herr, S. J., Vincent V. *Religious Psychology*. New York: Alba House, 1965.

Hill, Michael. *A Sociology of Religion*. New York: Basic Books, Inc., 1973.

Holbrook, Clyde A. *Religion, A Humanistic Field.* Englewood Cliffs, N.J.: Prentice-Hall, Inc., 1963.

Hooykaas, R. *Religion and the Rise of Modern Science.* London: Scottish Academic Press, 1972.

Ibn Khaldun. *The Muqquadimmah.* New York: Pantheon Books, 1958.

James, William. *The Varieties of Religious Experience.* New York: The New American Library, Inc., A Mentor Book, 1958.

Jeeves, Malcolm A. *Psychology and Christianity.* Donners Grove, Ill.: Inter Varsity Press, 1976.

Johnson, Paul E. *Psychology of Religion.* Nashville: Abingdon Press, 1959.

Jung, Carl Gustave. *Psychology and Religion.* New Haven: Yale University Press, 1977.

Kant, Immanuel. *Religion Within the Limits of Reason Alone.* La Salle, Ill.: Open Court, 1934.

Kilzer and Ross. *Western Social Thought.* Milwaukee: Bruce Publishing Company, 1954.

Kitagawa, Joseph M. "Introduction to the Life and Thought of Joachim Wach," *The Comparative Study of Religion, Joachim Wach.* New York: Columbia University Press, 1958.

Kraft, William. *The Search for the Holy.* Philadelphia: The Westminster Press, 1971.

Lenski, Gerard. *The Religious Factor.* Garden City, N.Y.: Doubleday & Co., 1961.

Lerner, Daniel. *The Human Meaning of the Social Sciences.* New York: Meridian Books, 1959.

Lessa, William A. and Evon Z. Vogt. *Reader in Comparative Religion.* New York: Harper and Row, Publishers, 1965.

Long, Charles H. "Human Centers: An Essay on Method in the History of Religions." *Soundings,* Fall, 1978, pp. 400-14.

Luckmann, Thomas. *The Invisible Religion.* New York: The Macmillan Co., 1967.

Macquarrie, John. *Principles of Christian Theology.* New York: Charles Scribner's Sons, 1966.

Mahdi, Muhsin. *Ibn Khaldun's Philosophy of History.* Chicago: University of Chicago Press, 1964.

Malinowski, Bronislaw. "Social and Individual Sources of Primitive Religion," *Religion, Society, and the Individual.* J. Milton Yinger, editor. New York: The Macmillan Co., 1957.

Malinowski, Bronislaw. *Myth in Primitive Psychology.* New York: W. W. Norton & Company, Inc., 1926.

Maloney, H. Newton, editor. *Current Perspectives in the Psychology of Religion.* Grand Rapids: William B. Eerdmans Publ. Co., 1977.

Marett, R. R. *Sacraments of Simple Folk.* Oxford: Clarendon Press, 1953.

Maslow, Abraham H. *Religions, Values and Peak-Experiences.* New York: The Viking Press, 1964.

Maslow, Abraham H. *Toward a Psychology of Being.* New York: D. Van Norstrand Co., 1968.

Maslow, Abraham H. *Motivation and Personality.* New York: Harper and Row, Publishers, 1970.

Meland, Bernard E. "The New Creation," *Process Theology.* Ewert H. Cousins, editor. New York: Newman Press, 1971.

Mellert, Robert B. *What is Process Theology?* New York: Paulist Press, 1975.

Moltmann, Jurgen with M. Douglas Meeks. "The Liberation of Oppressors," *Christianity and Crisis.* December 25, 1978, pp. 310-17.

Myrdal, Gunnar. "Notes on Facts and Evaluations." Appendix 2 in *An American Dilemma.* New York and London: Harper and Brothers, Publishers, 1944.

Nelson, Hart M., Raymond H. Potvin, and Joseph Shields. *The Religion of Children.* Washington, D.C.: United States Catholic Conference, 1977.

Nisbett, Robert. *The Social Philosophers.* New York: Washington Square Press, 1973.

Nouwen, Henri J. M. *Reaching Out: The Three Movements of the Spiritual Life.* Garden City, N.Y.: Doubleday and Co., Inc., 1975.

Oates, Wayne E. *The Psychology of Religion.* Waco: Word Books, Publisher, 1973.

O'Dea, Thomas F. *Sociology and the Study of Religion.* New York: Basic Books, Inc., 1970.

O'Dea, Thomas F. *The Sociology of Religion.* Englewood Cliffs, N.J.: Prentice Hall, Inc., 1966.

Oesterley, William Oscar Emil and Theodore H. Robinson. *An Introduction to the Books of the Old Testament.* London: S.P.C.K., 1934.

Ogden, Schubert M. "The Reality of God," *Process Theology.* Ewert H. Cousins, editor. New York: Newman Press, 1971.

O'Rourke, Kevin. "Are Institutions Obsolete?" *Review for Religions*, Vol. 29, No. 2, Mar. 1979, p. 246.

Panikkar, Raimundo. "The Ways of West and East," *New Dimensions in Religious Experience.* Proceedings of the College Theology Society, George Devine, editor. Staten Island: Alba House, 1971.

Parsons, Talcott. *Action Theory and the Human Condition.* New York: The Free Press, 1978.

Polanyi, M. *Personal Knowledge.* Chicago: University of Chicago Press, 1958.

Pruyser, Paul W. *A Dynamic Psychology of Religion.* New York: Harper and Row, Publishers, 1968.

Rader, Melvin and Bertram Jessup. *Art and Human Values.* Englewood Cliffs, N.J.: Prentice Hall, Inc., 1973.

Ramsey, Paul and John F. Wilson, Eds. *The Study of Religion in Colleges and Universities.* Princeton, N.J.: Princeton University Press, 1970.

Ritzer, H. *Sociology: A Multiple Paradigm Science.* Boston: Allyn and Bacon, 1974.

Reeder, John. "Religious Ethics as a Field and a Discipline." *The Journal of Religious Ethics*, Vol. 6, Spring 1978, pp. 32-53.

Schleiermacher, Friedrich. On Religion, *Speeches to its Cultured Despisers*. New York: Frederick Ungar Publishing Co., 1955.

Schleiermacher, Friedrich. *The Christian Faith*. Edinburgh: T. and T. Clark, 1928.

Schleiermacher, Friedrich. *Uber Die Religion* in *Samliche Werke* I. Berlin: Reinyer, 1843.

Schroeder, Widdick. *Cognitive Structures and Religious Research: Essays in Sociology and Theology*. East Lansing: Michigan State University Press, 1970.

Shorter, Aylward. "African Traditional Religion: Its Relevance in the Contemporary World," *Cross Currents*, Winter 1978/79, pp. 421-31.

Smart, Ninian. *The Religious Experience of Mankind*. New York: Charles Scribner's Sons, 1969.

Smith, Huston. "Do Drugs Have Religious Import," *Philosophy of Religion*. William L. Rowe and William J. Wainwright, editors. New York: Harcourt, Brace, Jovanovich, Inc., 1973.

Smith, Huston. "Drugs and Mysticism: An Analysis of the Relationship between Psychedelic Drugs and the Mystical Consciousness," a thesis presented to the Committee on Higher Degrees in History and Philosophy of Religion, Harvard University, June 1983.

Soundings, Summer, 1975. Especially art. by Susan Wittig, pp. 145-66. Special issue on structuralism.

Stace, Walter. "Subjectivity, Objectivity and the Self," *Philosophy of Religion*. William L. Rowe and William J. Wainwright, editors. New York: Harcourt, Brace, Jovanovich, Inc., 1973.

Stokes, Walter E. "A Whiteheadian Reflection on God's Relation to the World," *Process Theology.* Ewert H. Cousins, editor. New York: Newman Press, 1971.

Strunk, Jr., Orlo, editor. *Readings in the Psychology of Religion.* Nashville: Abingdon Press, 1959.

Strunk, Jr., Orlo. *Religion: A Psychological Interpretation.* New York: Abingdon Press, 1962.

Strunk, Jr., Orlo, editor. *The Psychology of Religion.* Nashville: Abingdon Press, 1971.

Temple, William. *Nature, Man and God.* (Gifford Lectures, 1932-34). New York: Macmillan Co., 1949.

Tillich, Paul. *Christianity and the Encounter of World Religions.* New York: Columbia University Press, 1964.

Timasheff, Nicolai. *Sociological Theory: Its Nature and Growth.* New York: Random House, 1957.

Turner, Victor. *Chihamba, The White Spirit: A Ritual Drama of the Ndembu.* Oxford: Manchester University Press, 1962.

Van der Leeuw, G. *Religion in Essence and Manifestation.* Vol. II. New York: Harper and Row, 1963.

van der Veken, Jan. "Structuralism and the Crisis of Humanism," *Religion in Life*, Spring, 1976, pp. 33-40.

Verhalen, Philip A. *Faith in a Secularized World.* New York: Paulist Press, 1976.

Vernon, Glen M. *Sociology of Religion.* New York: McGraw-Hill Book Co., Inc., 1962.

Wach, Joachim. *The Comparative Study of Religions.* New York: Columbia University Press, 1958.

Wach, Joachim. *The Sociology of Religion.* Chicago: The University of Chicago Press, 1944.

Wacker, Paulus G. "Christus Ohne Kirche?" *Theologie Und Glaube,* 64 (1974), pp. 1-28.

Wallace, Anthony F. C. *Religion and Anthropological View.* New York: Random House, 1966.

Whitehead, Alfred North. *Religion in the Making.* New York: The New American Library, Inc., Meridian Book, 1960.

Whitehead, Alfred N. "God and the World," *Process Theology.* Ewert H. Cousins, editor. New York: Newman Press, 1971.

Whitehead, Alfred North. "Immortality," *The Philosophy of Alfred North Whitehead.* (The Library of Living Philosophers, Vol. 3). Paul Arthur Schilpp, editor. Menasha: George Banta Publishing Co., 1941.

Whitehead, Alfred N. *Process and Reality.* New York: Macmillan Co., 1929.

Whitehead, Alfred North. *Science and the Modern World.* New York: Macmillan Co., 1926.

Wiebe, Donald. "Is a Science of Religion Possible?" *Studies in Religion/Sciences Religieuses,* Vol. 7, No. 1, 1978, pp. 5-17.

Williams, Daniel Day. *What Present Day Theologians are Thinking.*

Wilson, Monica. *Religion and the Transformation of Society.* Cambridge, England: Cambridge University Press, 1971.

Winch, Peter. *The Idea of a Social Science and its Relation to Philosophy.* London: Routledge and Paul; New York: Humanities Press, 1963.

Winter, Gibson. *Elements for a Social Ethic.* New York: Macmillan, 1966.

Yinger, J. Milton. *Religion, Society and the Individual.* New York: The Macmillan Co., 1957.

DATE DUE

HIGHSMITH   # 45220